REDEEMING HARD TIME
AND HARD TIMES

REDEEMING HARD TIME AND HARD TIMES

WHETHER YOU ARE BEHIND BARS OR BEHIND
THE EIGHT BALL, HARD TIMES ARE
TIMES TO GET CLOSE TO GOD

Judith Lawson PhD

Outskirts Press, Inc.
Denver, Colorado

The opinions expressed in this manuscript are solely the opinions of the author and do not represent the opinions or thoughts of the publisher. The author has represented and warranted full ownership and/or legal right to publish all the materials in this book.

Redeeming Hard Time and Hard Times
Whether you are behind bars or behind the eight ball, hard times are times to get close to God
All Rights Reserved.
Copyright © 2011 Judith Lawson PhD
v3.0 r1.0

Cover Photo © 2011 JupiterImages Corporation. All rights reserved - used with permission.

Scriptures from the Holy Bible, King James Version (KJV).

This book may not be reproduced, transmitted, or stored in whole or in part by any means, including graphic, electronic, or mechanical without the express written consent of the publisher except in the case of brief quotations embodied in critical articles and reviews.

Outskirts Press, Inc.
http://www.outskirtspress.com

ISBN: 978-1-4327-8119-4

Outskirts Press and the "OP" logo are trademarks belonging to Outskirts Press, Inc.

PRINTED IN THE UNITED STATES OF AMERICA

*To my daughter Cherie and my son-in-law Norby
whose prayers I am sure kept me alive and sane
through the worst of times.*

Table of Contents

Introduction..i

Part 1   **What is Christianity Anyway?**..................1

   Chapter 1   You Must Be Born Again..........................3
   Chapter 2   Winner or Loser: The Choice is Yours 11
   Chapter 3   My Dangerous Journey 19
   Chapter 4   Finding Mom 31
   Chapter 5   Finding God..41
   Chapter 6   Victory Takes Time................................57
   Chapter 7   Promises and Fiery Trials 71
   Chapter 8   Salt and Light..81

Part 2   **How Do We Come to Jesus?** 95

   Chapter 9   Coming to Jesus as Children 97
   Chapter 10   The Prodigal Son 105
   Chapter 11   Zoë Life 115
   Chapter 12   Aliens...125
   Chapter 13   The Inebriating Power of the World....133
   Chapter 14   Stinkin' Thinkin' 141
   Chapter 15   What is Forgiveness?..........................151

Part 3   **Spiritual Warfare**.....................................157

   Chapter 16   There's a War Going On! 159
   Chapter 17   Pulling Down Strongholds.................169
   Chapter 18   Cutting the Cords to the Past............181

Chapter 19	Pharmakeia	189
Chapter 20	Blessings Keep Devils Away	207
Chapter 21	Redeemed From the Curse	217
Chapter 22	Is Jesus the Only Way?	231
Chapter 23	Know So Hope	239
Chapter 24	The Rapture of the Church	245

Citations & Resources 259

Introduction

"Happy is he that hath the God of Jacob for his help, whose hope is in the Lord his God:
Which made heaven, and earth, the sea, and all that therein is: which keepeth truth forever:
Which executeth judgment for the oppressed: which giveth food to the hungry. The Lord looseth the prisoners:
The Lord openeth the eyes of the blind: the Lord raiseth them that are bowed down: the Lord loveth the righteous" (Psalms 146:5-8).

What comforting words from the Psalmist. He was speaking to Israel but he is also speaking to us today. He is speaking to the suffering, the afflicted, and the oppressed. God knows that we cannot cope with all of life's problems, responsibilities, and circumstances alone and it is the reason He sent His Son, Jesus to redeem us and carry our burdens for us.

Who are the righteous that the Lord loves? They, as you will learn in this book, are those who have cried out to Him in humility because God delights in those who are of a humble spirit. No matter what your circumstances, no matter who you are, no matter if you are serving hard time behind bars, or hard life situations have placed you behind the eight ball – in a very difficult situation where there seems to be no way out – Jesus is your answer. It is the Lord who looses us from our oppressions.

Redeem the Time

The Apostle Paul, in his letter to the Church in the ancient city of Colosse talks about redeeming the time. As a chapel preacher for the men at the Tampa Bay Teen Challenge International I presented them with the challenge of redeeming their time – their court ordered time in that rehabilitation facility. The choice before them, and you, is to either simply spend this time, or use it to draw near to God. Drawing near to God will cause Him to draw near to you and change your life for good.

"Draw nigh to God, and He will draw nigh to you" (James 4:8a).

Now, I am going to challenge you to do the same. I also presented the men with several Bible teachings of important topics that are relevant for those who are incarcerated, have recently been incarcerated or for those who are in a drug, alcohol, or some other kind of rehabilitation center awaiting reentry into the world. This book is a collection of those teachings which will help prisoners to use their time of incarceration to grow spiritually and deepen their relationship with the Lord Jesus Christ.

Many Kinds of Prisons

I have never been incarcerated, but I have been a prisoner.

When you are bound by devils, you are in a prison that can be worse than incarceration. Perhaps your prison is depression, or mental illness, or loneliness. There are many kinds of prisons. You can be in the outside world but bound, like I was, but when you are truly free, no matter how many armed guards, sally ports, or rolling barbed wire fences surround you, you are free indeed.

"And ye shall know the truth, and the truth shall make you free" (John 8:32).

"If the Son therefore shall make you free, ye shall be free indeed" (John 8:36).

Life is difficult when you are locked up, court ordered to a rehabilitation facility, and or compelled to be in custody in some way. But to face life on the outside can be even more difficult if you are not prepared. These teachings have been written and compiled to do just that, prepare the inmate to be able to confront the challenges that lie ahead.

In Plain Language

Although there are many inmates who are extremely intelligent, and many who have solid educations, there are also those who have not had the privilege of a college or seminary education. Therefore, I have written and preached these teachings, not with theological terms that would be difficult to understand for these precious brothers and sisters but in plain, everyday language – conversational English – that will be easily comprehended, and easily applied to everyday life.

Each of these teachings were intended to stand alone so

some of them may be found to be a bit repetitive but biblical principles will be found in each one. Reading the Bible is one thing, but having the ability to apply its principles is quite another. Hopefully these teachings will accomplish just that.

It is my desire that this book finds its way into the hands of many incarcerated men and women who wish to redeem their time, and anyone else who has a deep hunger for the Word of God whose desire it is to become free in the spirit if not in the flesh. Satan has been robbing you long enough. In John 10:10 we are told:

"The thief (Satan) cometh not, but for to steal, and to kill, and to destroy: I am come that they might have life, and that they might have it more abundantly" (John 10:10).

My prayer for you is that you become freer than you have ever been, even if you have been destined to spend some years of your life in prison, because Jesus Christ is the one who sets the captives free. Those who are free in their spirit are truly free indeed.

"The Spirit of the Lord GOD is upon me; because the LORD hath anointed Me to preach good tidings to the poor; He hath sent me to bind up the brokenhearted, to proclaim liberty to the captives, and the opening of the prison to them that are bound;

To proclaim the acceptable year of the LORD, and the day of vengeance of our God; to comfort all that mourn;

To appoint unto them that mourn in Zion, to give unto them beauty for ashes, the oil of joy for mourning, the garment of praise for the spirit of heaviness; that they might be called trees of righteousness, the planting of the LORD, that He may be glorified.

And they shall build the old wastes, they shall raise up the former desolations, and they shall repair the waste cities, the desolations of many generations" (Isaiah 61:1-4).

Enjoy the journey,
Dr. Judy Lawson

Part 1
What is Christianity Anyway?

CHAPTER 1

You Must Be Born Again

The New Birth

THE BIBLE TELLS us that we must be born again. But what does that mean and why did God tell us that we must be born again? Let's see how the Bible answers those questions.

1. In the Bible, a man asked Jesus how he could be born again because it is impossible to enter a second time into his mother's womb!

    "Jesus answered and said to him, verily, verily, I say unto thee, except a man be born again, he cannot see the Kingdom of God" (John 3:3).

    "That which is born of the flesh is flesh; and that which is born of the Spirit is spirit. Marvel not that I said unto thee, ye must be born again" (John 3:6, 7).

2. But why is the new birth required? Aren't there many ways to heaven? This is what Jesus said:

"I am the Way, the Truth and the Life; no man cometh unto the Father, but by Me" (John 14:6).

"But if we walk in the light as He is in the light, we have fellowship one with another, and the blood of Jesus Christ His Son cleanseth us from all sin.
If we say that we have no sin, we deceive ourselves, and the truth is not in us. If we confess our sins, He is faithful and just to forgive us our sins and to cleanse us from all unrighteousness.
If we say that we have not sinned, we make Him a liar, and His word is not in us" (1 John 1:7-10).

"But God commendeth His love toward us, in that, while we were yet sinners, Christ died for us" (Romans 5:8).

3. **Well, if what Jesus Christ did for us on the cross and if His blood is what cleanses us all from all sin, why isn't everyone saved? Are there only certain people who can get saved?**

"For whoever shall call upon the name of the Lord shall be saved" (Romans 10:13).

4. **Well, what about all the good things I've done during my life, I've probably done more good things than bad. Doesn't that help me get into heaven?**

"For by grace are ye saved through faith; and that not of yourselves; it is the gift of God.
Not of works, lest any man should boast." (Ephesians 2:8-9).

5. **Why do we have to get our sins cleansed? Does everyone sin? What happens to us if we don't get our sins cleansed?**

   "For all have sinned and come short of the glory of God" (Romans 3:23).

   "For the wages of sin is death; but the gift of God is eternal life through Jesus Christ our Lord" (Romans 6:23).

6. **How will I know when I have been born again? Will I change?**

   "Therefore, if any man be in Christ, he is a new creature; old things are passed away; behold, all things are become new" (2 Corinthians 5:17).

7. **Okay, what do I have to do to experience this new birth so I can be sure of being saved?**

   "Behold, I stand at the door and knock; if any man hear My voice and open the door, I will come in to him and sup (fellowship) with him, and he with Me" (Revelation 3:20).

How to be Born Again or Rededicate Your Life to Christ

Has the Lord been knocking on the door of your heart? Has He been inviting you to get saved or, if you were saved as a child, to rededicate your life to Him? If so, the following will help you to enter into a personal relationship with Him.

1. Accept God's Word that He loves you and wants to give you an abundant life.

2. Accept God's Word that you are a sinner and that this separates you from God and that you must truly repent and turn away from all sin.

3. Accept God's Word that says the shed blood of Jesus is God's only provision for man to get rid of sin.

4. Accept God's Word that Jesus Christ is our only way to have contact with God.

5. Open the door of your heart and invite Him in. Receive Jesus Christ as your Savior and Lord. Don't hold anything back. Invite Him to come into every area of your life.

Open The Door of Your Heart with This Prayer:

Lord Jesus, I have never really let You into every area of my heart and life before today, but now I realize that I need to do just that. I realize that I need You because I have done wrong and I have rejected You. I want to confess my sins to You and ask You to forgive me. I forgive others, not by feelings but by my choice. I truly repent of all my sins and turn my back on my old life. With an act of my will I receive You into my heart as my Lord and Savior. Please take control of the mess I have made of my life and change me Lord. Help me to live the life You intended me to live.
    Please, dear Lord, reveal to me Your plan for my life. I have walked in my plan that has been a failure long enough.

Help me to walk in Your ways while I am alive and take me to heaven to be with You for all eternity when I die. I thank You Lord Jesus for coming into my life and saving my soul. Thank You Lord that I am now a born again Christian. Amen.

You may feel the presence of God at this moment and you might even "feel" saved. But you may not feel that way later. That is why it is important that you stand on faith; faith that if Jesus said He would come in and save you He did just that. Faith that even if you don't "feel" saved, you still are because He said so.

Now, it is important that you continue to thank the Lord for your salvation and it is also important that you get into the Word.

You've Got Mail

Start reading your Bible and read it every day. It is God's love letter to you. Many of you in prison get very little mail; well Jesus has a letter for you every day if only you would read it. There are many letters in the New Testament, and guess what – they were written by a prisoner, the Apostle Paul. Even if you don't understand it at first, continue to read it anyway. Picture, if you will in your mind, putting a basket under a water faucet and the water going right through it. The water may be going through the basket, but the basket is getting clean. You see, the Bible is not just a book; it is the Holy Spirit of God going into your spirit to clean it and to cleanse your mind as well.

Pray every day and praise God for everything – even the bad things – because praising God has a way of redeeming circumstances right out of the devil's hand. Seek out the fellowship of other prisoners who are born again. You will be amazed at how many there are. Start praying and studying God's Word together with other Christians because it will make you all strong in your spirit.

In Romans 10: 9 and 10 we see that it is not enough for you to just believe it in your heart; you must say it with your mouth as well.

"That if thou shalt confess with thy mouth the Lord Jesus, and shalt believe in thine heart that God hath raised Him from the dead, thou shalt be saved.

For with the heart man believeth unto righteousness; and with the mouth confession is made unto salvation" (Romans 10:9, 10).

So, you see, believing in your heart and confessing it with your mouth is the pathway to salvation. However, God doesn't stop there, He is willing; not only to save your soul, and redeem you from your enemies (physical and spiritual) He also wants to deliver you into a new and wonderful place in life.

"Let the redeemed of the Lord say so, whom He hath redeemed from the hand of the enemy;

And gathered them out of the lands, from the east, and from the west, from the north, and from the south.

They wandered in the wilderness in a solitary way; they found no city to dwell in.

Hungry and thirsty, their soul fainted in them.

Then they cried unto the LORD in their trouble, and He delivered them out of their distresses

And He led them forth by the right way that they might go to a city of habitation.

Oh that men would praise the Lord for His goodness, and for His wonderful works to the children of men!

For He satisfieth the longing soul, and filleth the hungry soul with goodness.

Such as sit in darkness and in the shadow of death, being bound in affliction and iron;

Because they rebelled against the Words of God, and condemned the counsel of the most High.

Therefore He brought down their heart with labour; they fell down, and there was none to help.

Then they cried unto the Lord in their trouble, and He saved them out of their distresses.

He brought them out of darkness and the shadow of death, and brake their bands in sunder" (Psalm 107:2-14).

You have wandered alone in the wilderness long enough because of your rebellion. He will lead you in the right way if only you cry out to Him, so begin to praise Him. Be a witness to all the others. Let the light of Jesus shine through you now that you are a child of God and begin your new journey through the Word of God. Enjoy these teachings, they were written just for you.

CHAPTER **2**

Winner or Loser: The Choice is Yours

Learning How to be a Winner

LIFE IS FULL of choices - one of them being whether we will have the mentality of a winner or of a loser and another choice being whether we will allow the Lord Jesus Christ or the devil to have the most influence in our lives. It is important that you know about the devil, and the fact that he is your enemy and that God has not left you helpless against him. God has given you weapons but unless you know your enemy, what those weapons are, and how to use them effectively, you will be a loser and a victim and you will be defeated.

Our most powerful weapon is the Bible, the Word of God. It is not just a book; it is the very breath of God. It is referred to as a two edged sword. One of those edges is getting the Word into your spirit and the other edge is allowing it to come out of your mouth as you speak the Word and applying what it says to your life.

"For the Word of God is quick, and powerful, and sharper than any two edged sword, piercing even to the dividing asunder of soul and spirit, and of the joints and marrow, and is a discerner of the thoughts and intents of the heart" (Hebrews 4:12).

When you learn how to use the weapons of spiritual warfare effectively it will help you to get free and stay free and become a winner rather than a loser in life.

I am passionate about teaching you how to be aware of demonic influences that we all feel in our lives and the fact that there is something we can do about them. You see, God's Word teaches us that as long as we are to remain upon the earth we will be engaged in spiritual warfare with Satan, the enemy of our souls. If you are incarcerated you probably don't have to be convinced that the devil is real; perhaps you have felt the presence of evil all around you.

The Devil Made Me Do It!

One of the important things we learn when we become children of God is that we need to own our faults. We can't just say the devil made me do it. Therefore, it is important to point out that we must take care not to blame demonic forces for every uncomfortable situation or flaw in our character. We must, however, learn about spiritual warfare because demonic activity is a major reason Christians have so many perplexing problems in their lives. Sadly, spiritual warfare is a key ingredient that is not emphasized in the Church today.

It is true, Jesus defeated the enemy at Calvary; however, the mental knowledge that Jesus defeated the devil and that we have authority over him isn't enough. Many continually allow

Satan, whom we know was defeated, to beat them down, push them around and take advantage of them. They forget that Jesus did not make them losers, but winners!

Although we might be strong believers in setting people free from demonic bondage, we must also always be mindful that spiritual warfare should never be an end in itself, but a means to an end. As we strive to bring balance to this much-neglected ministry we must attempt to avoid either over emphasizing spiritual warfare, seeing demons everywhere, or under emphasizing it with the idea that any acknowledgement of Satan is an invitation for demonic activity. It is not true that if you don't bother him he won't bother you, bothering you is his job!

You're In the Army Now!

Our victory over our enemy, Satan, has never been in question. The war was won, once and for all. What Christ did on the cross was for all time and for all people if they will accept it. We are not to fear the enemy but become knowledgeable about his activities so that we will be able to walk in victory. Military strategists involve their troops in learning even the minutest details about the enemy they will be facing. They go into battle well prepared and they know what to expect when they arrive on the battlefield. We can be certain that Satan knows us. We are his enemies and he knows us quite well. He is continually arming himself with information about us. Spiritual warfare is constant, Satan never lets up. The war is being waged against us 24 hours a day, 7 days a week. Satan never calls in sick! He is relentless in his attempts to put a stop to and curtail the work of God in us and through us. When we are ignorant of his devices, however, he has the upper hand. It is the ignorance of the believer that is the devil's only real power against us.

"Therefore my people are gone into captivity, because they have no knowledge" (Isaiah 5:13a).

"My people are destroyed for lack of knowledge" (Hosea 4:6a).

Sin, the Devil's Open Door

Sin is the main reason the devil's evil spirits have been given a legal right to enter a life to torment and harass, but there are other reasons as well. In some instances a legal right may have been given to the enemy by the sins of the parents or by the curses from former generations, accidents, traumatic experiences, or the actions of other people. The devil is a great opportunist and he does not miss a chance to hurt and discredit God and His children. When we open the door to the Lord, He comes in, but then we need to close the doors that have been opened to the devil. You need to remove those legal rights and entry points and close those doors for good.

Spiritual warfare is not just a fragment of Christianity; it is the whole of the Christian experience. It encompasses everything we do. To be a Christian is to be a spiritual warrior. To be a spiritual warrior is to walk consistently and victoriously through life with the Lord Jesus Christ. Let me encourage you to see for yourself. Go get your Bible and follow along by reading all the Scripture references I cite.

Who Are You?

Do you really know who you are? I didn't before I knew the Lord. I thought I was a loser. It was a process that took time, but after reading and studying the Word of God I slowly began to understand where I came from, who I was in Christ, and where I was going. I began to realize that the choice was mine – did I want to accept the loser mentality or did I want to think like a winner so that I could be one?

The reason for this testimony and compilation of teachings in this book is to help you realize who Jesus is, who Satan is and who YOU are in Christ so that you are able to engage the enemy and gain the victory. You must, however, belong to Him before you can know who you are in Him.

Okay, now that you know something about spiritual warfare, and if you have indeed become a born again Christian and belong to God, you are ready to read some of the teachings I have gathered together for you. We have now reached the part of this book that contains them. So sit back and imagine that I am there with you preaching and teaching because each one of these teachings was given in front of a group of people who were going through much of the same things you are going through in your life right now.

Hopefully you will laugh with me and cry with me as we go through these teachings that I have received from the Lord. I have included my testimony in this book and intertwined so that you will know who I am, where I came from and why I am able to relate to you the way I do. I have a heart for the prisoner and have used my story to show many of them what God is capable of doing in a person's life when he or she makes the decision to not only come to Him, but to lay life down and live for Him. Whatever you think of yourself, you have value, you are important to God and you have a future. I preached to the men at Teen Challenge bringing hope to them, I visit the women in our county jail weekly to counsel them and bring them hope, and it is my desire that as you read this book it will bring hope to you as well.

Living Successfully

I am here to help you get free and stay free. Oh, I'm not going to help you escape from that place – but I am going to help you escape from a worse place. Yes, a worse place. It is called hell and that is a place you never want to go. I am going to help you learn how to stay out of that place called hell and be free spiritually. There is good news and bad news about the devil. The good news is that the devil has been confined to live in one small area of the universe – earth. The bad news is we have to live here too! However, I want to teach you how to live successfully in spite of that. Thank goodness, this is only temporary because we only have to live here while we are in our bodies.

You see, we are three part beings. The real substance of who we are is our spirit. Our mind, emotions, senses, and feelings are our soul. Our body—well actually it only carries the real us around while we are temporarily on the earth. It is our earth suit. We can only get here by being born inside our earth suit. When we die and lose our earth suit, we can't stay here any longer. If we are born again and belong to God, we will go to be with Him when our earth suit wears out or for some other reason can no longer sustain life. To be absent from the body is to be present with the Lord.

"Now He that hath wrought us for the selfsame thing is God, who also hath given unto us the earnest (the down payment) of the Spirit.

Therefore we are always confident, knowing that, whilst we are at home in the body, we are absent from the Lord:

(For we walk by faith, not by sight)

We are confident, I say, and willing rather to be absent from the body, and to be present with the Lord" (2 Corinthians 5:5-8).

If we are not born again, however, and we don't listen and obey the truth of God, we will listen to a lie and yes...you guessed it, we go to be with our father the devil, the father of lies.

God is Not Your Father Unless You Are Born Again

Most people think that we are all children of God automatically but that's not what God says!

"Jesus said unto them, if God were your Father, ye would love Me, for I proceeded forth and came from God; neither came I of Myself, but He sent Me.

Why do ye not understand my speech? Even because ye cannot hear My word.

Ye are of your father the devil, and the lusts of your father ye will do. He was a murderer from the beginning; and abode not in the truth, because there is no truth in him. When he (Satan) speaketh a lie, he speaketh of his own: for he is a liar and the father of it" (John 8:42-44).

Be an Overcomer

Since God is my Father, I am an overcomer. The Bible

says that the testimony of what Jesus Christ has done for us in our lives is very powerful indeed. So you see it is through my testimony that I have become an overcomer. I am sharing with you what God has done in my life in the hope that you will learn that a relationship with the Lord Jesus Christ is the only way to an overcoming life for you as well.

"And they overcame him (Satan) by the blood of the Lamb, and by the word of their testimony" (Revelation 12:11).

You will also learn that this Christianity thing is not some magic bullet and can sometimes be hard work. Your spirit gets saved immediately when you cry out to God in humility and sincerity but becoming free in your soul, which is comprised of your mind and emotions, doesn't all happen overnight and sometimes isn't easy. But I can assure you, it IS well worth it.

"Wherefore, my beloved, as ye have always obeyed, not as in my presence only, but now much more in my absence, work out your own salvation with fear and trembling" (Philippians 2:12).

I can assure you that as you work out your salvation you will see that you are an overcoming winner because Jesus Christ is a winner and you belong to Him.

CHAPTER 3

My Dangerous Journey

I AM THE Administrator for the Degree Completion Program and occasional Professor at a Christian College in Central Florida and have earned six college degrees that include two doctorates: a Doctor of Ministry and a Doctor of Philosophy in Divinity. I am also a Chaplain at the Pasco County Florida Jail and counsel the women there. In addition to all that, I also work with some drug rehabilitation ministries in my area. If you could look me over today, you'd probably be thinking to yourself…She has Seminary Doctorates, she's a college administrator. She looks like she has never seen a hard day in her life. Well, you know that old saying; don't judge a book by its cover? You see the reason I tell my testimony is because I am a totally different person than I was before I knew God. The person I was is now dead and if you are born again, the old you is also dead. You are a new person in Christ.

Deadly Deception

I wasn't always a Christian. I was in my 30's when many years ago in an attempt to contact and communicate with my deceased mother's spirit, I got into spiritism and witchcraft. Like most who have journeyed into the tangled web of witchcraft, I never doubted the existence of a supernatural, unseen realm. Actually, a part of me seemed to exist there. I was born on the proverbial day of witches and hobgoblins, Halloween. Yes, my story begins on Halloween in Cleveland, Ohio. Not only was I born on that day, but it was also my parent's third wedding anniversary making this a very celebrated day at our house. I know...who gets married on Halloween? Go figure. My father's nickname for me was "Bugaboo" a name I later learned means evil spirit - no wonder I had problems. We need to be careful about nicknames. If they are derogatory they can stick and cause a door to be opened for the enemy to come into one's life and harass them.

From the time I can remember I felt rejected and lonely and although I wore an outgoing, gregarious façade, underneath was the turmoil of a layered, schizophrenic personality of rejection and rebellion. Religious training for my brother and me consisted of a few catechism lessons in the Catholic Church so we could make our first communion and confirmation. I never did know just what it all meant. There was never a Bible in our home but because my mother taught me how to pray I always believed in and had the fear of God in me. Knowing very little about Him led me to believe that whoever He was He didn't seem to be very interested in me.

From as far back as I can remember it felt as though I was living in two separate dimensions. Even as a small child I would have strange psychic experiences that I didn't understand. My exposure and involvement in these occurrences would often leave me feeling that I had somehow entered a

PART 1: WHAT IS CHRISTIANITY ANYWAY?

supernatural realm. This, combined with my Halloween birth, made me believe I was "called" by God to some special, high calling and when I became an adult, a troubled one at that, I thought I had been "called" to be a witch. Now mind you, I thought a witch was the highest spiritual "calling" by God upon one's life. Boy was I deceived. But it would be years, and many trials and tribulations later when I would realize how deceived I really had been.

Called

My parents were wed on Halloween day, 1935.
    I was born on Halloween day, 1938.
A mere coincidence you might say,
    but I thought it was fate.

Having been born on Halloween Day,
    Was I called to be a witch?
I studied the craft quite seriously,
    convinced I'd found my niche.

What I found instead was evil and death,
    destruction at every turn.
Paranoid fear overtook my soul
    the more that I would learn.

Soon, by darkness I was possessed.
    Insanity ruled my way.
The voices were driving me over the edge
    Would I see my next birthday?

(cont.)

They informed me this was the way to God,
    my calling manifest.
That spirits would lead me to God someday.
    I would be dead by then I'd guessed!

Then, someone told me the truth at last…
    "Ask Jesus into your heart," she said.
"He'll take the mess you've made
    and give you life instead!"

Bea Rake knew God, she said she did;
    I could tell she knew Him quite well.
She said she'd been into witchcraft
    and that it surely led to hell!

"Do you have a Bible?
    Read Exodus 22:18."
I read the words upon the page
    I was shocked as to what I had seen!

Do not allow a witch to live…
    The words pierced my very soul!
No wonder I was dying
    and my life out of control.

There happened to be a miracle service
    at a nearby local church.
She took me there one night in May.
    Where Jesus ended my search!

He welcomed me with outstretched arms
    As I lifted my hands to His.
He assured me things would be all right
    that He always Was and Is.

> "About that calling on your life," He said…
> "You've surely been beguiled.
> You've not been called to be a witch…
> you've been called to be my child!"
>
> JL

Keep Your Eyes on the Prize

The Apostle Paul tells us in Philippians 3:13 and 14 not to look back. We are to forget those things which are behind us and reach forward, toward the prize of the high calling of God in Christ Jesus. So, no matter how tough it gets, we are to keep our eyes on the prize.

"Brethren, I count not myself to have apprehended (to have grasped and understood everything): but this one thing I do, forgetting those things which are behind, and reaching forth unto those things which are before
I press toward the mark for the prize of the high calling of God in Christ Jesus" (Philippians 3:13, 14).

In this portion of Scripture, the Apostle Paul sees himself as a runner in a race. He is pressing on with everything he's got so that he won't fall short of the goal Jesus has set for him. We, too, must be that determined to reach our goal because there are all sorts of distractions, temptations, and worldly things that get in the way and threaten our relationship with God and our ability to finish well. It's not where you came from that will count in the end, but where you are going and finishing well that is the prize. Perhaps my testimony will encourage you to continue to walk in the ways of the Lord and to reach for the prize of that new life in Him that He promised you as well.

Dangerous Journey

As a small child, my mother taught me how to pray. You know the prayer:

> "Now I lay me down to sleep,
> I pray the Lord my soul to keep.
> If I should die before I wake,
> I pray the Lord my soul to take."

That is actually a salvation prayer so I believe I belonged to God way back then, I just didn't know it. I was an intercessor at a very young age and prayed to God often. I would cry myself to sleep praying for the children in Europe who had been caught in the ravages of war and also for my two loving uncles who were soldiers in World War II.

When I was about 8 years old, I was raped in my own bed one night by another uncle who wasn't so loving. He and my aunt stayed overnight because he went out and got so drunk he couldn't drive home. From that point on, my life was never the same. I obviously took in many evil spirits from that traumatic incident. It caused me to have a lot of emotional issues. I never told a soul about what happened and I am convinced that children take in a mute spirit that keeps them from being able to speak about the incident, thus making it easier for that demon of rape to continue its dirty work in the child's life. I have often wondered how differently my life would have turned out had my innocence not been robbed from me that night.

Although I didn't know it for several years, I had inherited witch spirits from my paternal grandmother and great grandmother. They were both alcoholics and they were both psychic. I only met that grandmother twice in my life and she was crazy. Undoubtedly she got that way from the witchcraft. That is what witchcraft will do to you; you'll either go crazy or you'll die. The combination of this inheritance and trauma from the rape were causing me to become very oppressed by Satan. Perhaps you have been through some trauma in your life and have also inherited some unclean spirits. That may be why you have done some of the things you have done. We don't only inherit physically, we inherit spiritually as well.

The Man of My Dreams

I was a high school drop out at the age of 16 and went to work as a receptionist and by the time I was 18 I was married to a man I had only known for five months. I thought he was the man of my dreams but our marriage was turning out to be a nightmare instead. It was stormy from the beginning. My husband drank too much and spent most of his time and money in bars which kept us poor. He was 6 years older than I, had been in the Navy and around the world. I was a teenager, had never left the state of Ohio and was too naïve to even know what an alcoholic was. Our marriage was doomed from the beginning.

The drinking and money problems were only the tip of the iceberg. Those were years of deep depression, rejection and loneliness.

My Precious Babies

We had three children in the first four years and were carrying more responsibility than we could handle. I was pregnant all during my 18th and 19th years. At 22 I gave birth to the third child. Even though my marriage was not doing well and I was so young, I was a good mother and dearly loved my babies and loved taking care of them. However, I did not want to have another child. My Cherie, Bobby and Scotty were all I could handle. Well, at age 24 I got pregnant anyway with a fourth child. Another reason I did not want another child was because, not only were we incompatible in marriage, but our blood types were incompatible as well. My blood type was Type O RH Negative and my husband's was Type B RH Positive. A baby has a 50/50 chance of inheriting the father's blood type and if that happens, there are problems. We had been fortunate with three healthy babies but this one inherited his father's positive blood type. This particular combination causes a positive baby to be rejected in a negative mother like a foreign object or like a transplanted organ would be. Only weeks into the pregnancy I knew something was wrong. I fell very ill as my body worked hard to slough off all the dead blood cells and I felt a strong sense of foreboding; both our lives were in danger. I knew tragedy was on the horizon and that this baby would be born either retarded or dead. You see, it is the red blood cells that carry oxygen to the brain and with my body killing off the baby's red blood cells, there would be brain damage for sure. All during the pregnancy I was preparing for either scenario.

I told the doctors I knew this baby would be born dead. This was yet another psychic phenomenon, along with many others I continued to have through the years. This was something I couldn't have known with normal senses, but with this so called sixth sense, I did.

Of course the doctors didn't believe me, but after about

six months, my baby stopped moving and I knew he had died. The doctors said no, but I knew better. They didn't have the technology they have today. But I was right; after carrying him for eight months, my precious baby boy was born dead. Carrying death around in my body for two months took a toll on me physically and emotionally and I nearly died as well.

Just a few years after the trauma of having given birth to a stillborn child my husband and I finally separated. Shortly after that I suffered another trauma when he simply left and deserted me to raise the three children on my own. His whereabouts were unknown for several years. The children were only five, seven and eight years old.

It was Us against the World

Although home was a much more peaceful place without the arguments and chaos since my husband was gone, I had no idea of how we would survive. I had no money, no job, no training, and was a high school dropout. My dad helped for a while but then moved out of state. So, we ended up in government housing. That's a nice way of saying "the projects," otherwise known as the ghetto.

I went on welfare and picked up a few jobs in nightclubs working till all hours of the night. Then the welfare people told me I could go to college on a welfare grant. I was very sorry I had quit school and really wanted badly to go to college some day. So, I did what I had to do to enroll in the local Community College.

I was able to get through one year but between taking care of three kids singlehandedly, the stress of living in the projects, and working till all hours of the night, I was pretty much burning the candle at both ends. I had to figure out how to do it all. Well, I was in the right neighborhood because all I had to do is begin asking some questions and it didn't take me long to discover where I could obtain some help. Yes, I learned that I could do it all with a little help from my friends, those little friends that came in bottles that is – Amphetamines.

The government project we lived in was a dangerous place! Before we even got completely moved in, some neighbor kids had already broken in and stolen some things. I worried all the time that someone would break in again, and maybe hurt us. I was coming home at two and three o'clock in the morning from work and that was no place to be walking to your apartment at that time of night. Carrying a hand gun was not an option but a necessity. Thank God I never had to use it.

Up until this time we owned a nice ranch home in the suburbs so you can imagine how traumatic this move was. Not being able to afford the payments after my husband left I had to sell the house and because we only owned it for a few years I made only enough money from the sale to buy a car with which to get back and forth to work. I tried unsuccessfully to find a place in a better neighborhood, but had no choice but to move into government housing because it was all I could afford. Living here in the projects felt like we had gone to hell. This is the time in my life when I really started crying out to God in desperation

Everyone has their bottom, well I was reaching mine. I knew we did not belong here, but I had no choice. I especially worried about my daughter. Amazingly, God was watching out for us but especially her, since she was such a beautiful teenager and so vulnerable. One of the kids in the neighborhood took it upon himself to protect her. He was a six-foot giant of a young man, black as the night and sweet hearted as they come. Every time a dangerous crowd of thugs blocked the way to our apartment threatening her, Tiny would just show up from seemingly out of nowhere and the gang would scatter. They didn't mess with Tiny.

So, here we were - I had lost my baby, my husband, my house, the support of my parents, and forced to move from our suburban home into the ghetto. My kids and I were not street smart and were traumatized. My parents got divorced after 27 years of marriage, my father moved out of state; my mother got remarried and was preoccupied with her new husband so there was no help from anywhere.

Things Couldn't Possibly Get Any Worse... or Could They?

Well, they did. I could not believe it when the doctor came out of surgery and told us that there was nothing else he could do. My beautiful, 57 year old mother, who had been diagnosed with pancreatic cancer, had only three months to live. In exactly three months, she was gone.

After the funeral I began having visions and dreams of her lying in that coffin. I looked very much like her and suddenly, in my dreams, it would be me lying there. Where did she go I repeatedly asked myself and where would I have gone if I would have died? Surely we both would go to heaven; after all, we are good people and never robbed a bank or killed anyone. I began to wonder what it was that makes it possible for people to go to heaven and not hell anyway? Is being a good person going to get me there? Those were the questions that were tormenting my mind.

Needless to say, I was an emotional train wreck by this time. My life had been turned upside down. It had been comprised of trauma, after trauma, and crisis, after crisis. Are you getting the picture, not only of my life here, but perhaps of yours as well? Think about it. How many crises and traumas have you suffered through? Even the ones you caused; even they are still traumas.

The relationship between my mother and I had always been strained, but at that point in my life, I felt my mother was the only one who even half loved me and hadn't completely rejected me. Consequently, I was having extreme difficulty handling her untimely death. I was so troubled that I visited a psychiatric clinic to see if I could get some help with sorting things out. During the visit I kept trying to tell the doctor about how troubled I was over my mother's death but he insisted I tell him what drugs I was on. I guess my being a junkie was more obvious than I thought. He wasn't listening to a word I said. Instead, he proceeded to write out two prescriptions for more drugs and bid me farewell. I told him I was an addict and he gave me two prescriptions for more drugs. Hello! Even I knew that the last thing I needed was more drugs. As I walked down the hallway of that clinic thinking that the doctor was the one who was the nut, I tore the prescriptions up and came to the conclusion there was no help for me here. How would I ever be able to cope with the death of my mom?

CHAPTER 4

Finding Mom

Looking in All the Wrong Places

I WAS HAVING extreme difficulty coping with the death of my mother. First, I lost her because she divorced my dad and went off with another man and now she was dead and I lost her for the second time. I had no one to talk to. My family would not come to the projects to visit for fear they would get attacked, so I felt they had all abandoned me. The psychiatrist at the clinic wouldn't even listen.

My mom was so young and beautiful; I could not believe that she had actually died and that I would never see her or speak to her again. If you have had this, or a similar experience, then you know how one doesn't really comprehend the finality of the death of a loved one until it happens to you. For months I would pick up the phone to call her and suddenly be faced with the realization that she was no longer there. I missed my mom so much and longed to have her in my life once again. I loved her so much and now I had no one to turn to.

I began to rationalize that if I couldn't talk with my mother directly, perhaps it would be possible to communicate with her spirit. I had never doubted the concept of life after death and had read many articles on the subject. After all, I felt I had been "called of God" and born with psychic powers so, I rationalized that it should be possible to learn how to do that. I had put my supernatural abilities on the back burner of my life for so long, and now, I decided, it was time to begin developing these powers and abilities once again.

Two Sources of the Supernatural

I was always under the impression that the supernatural psychic phenomena that I had experienced from childhood was all from God. I wondered who He was and if He could really be found somehow. I had asked myself that question a million times. Or is it the other way around, I wondered, can I be found by God. Who is He anyway? Why did I have this nagging feeling inside of me that I had been "called" by Him? What did that mean? All I knew is that I felt very close to the supernatural realm.

I had no knowledge of the fact that there are two sources of the supernatural: God and Satan. I was an avid reader of several books on the subject so I knew that some people had allegedly communicated with the dead. Sadly, the world doesn't tell you about the consequences of dabbling in this ancient art the Bible calls necromancy - I had to find that out the hard way.

It wasn't long before I decided to quit college and devote all my time to studying the occult with a passion. I read every book I could find on the new age religion, witchcraft, reincarnation, Wicca, Zen, Buddhism, Hinduism, Rosicrucianism, and Free Masonry, just to name a few. I learned about the various ways of fortune telling and divining and tried them all. It didn't take me long to discover that I was very talented in these areas and began telling fortunes and giving people life readings where I would tell them who they had been reincarnated from in their former lives. I would learn later that all these areas of religion are false and of the devil himself. They are lures to draw people into Satan's web of lies and deceit and rather than draw you closer to God they drive you further away from Him instead. God addresses the issue of reincarnation in the Bible.

"And as it is appointed unto men once to die, but after this the judgment" (Hebrews 9:27).

Contact Between Living and Dead Prohibited by God

God has given us stern warnings in the Bible on the issue of attempting to contact the dead or other spirits such as angels or saints. His commands to us on these subjects are unwavering, in fact God clearly tells us that it is not possible for us to contact our deceased loved ones, and that there are great spiritual dangers lurking for those who attempt to do so.

"And beside all this, between us and you there is a great gulf fixed; so that they which would pass from hence to you cannot; neither can they pass to us, that would come from thence" (Luke 16:26).

In this portion of Scripture God makes it very clear that He does not allow the living to communicate with the dead, or the dead to communicate with the living. This story in the book of Luke is of two men in eternity. It teaches us that there is a great gulf fixed between the saved and the lost in eternity, so that they cannot come together and there is also a great gulf fixed between the living and the dead. God forbids any attempt of the living to contact the dead

> "There shall not be found among you any one that maketh his son or his daughter to pass through the fire, or that useth divination, or an observer of times (astrology), or an enchanter, or a witch.
> Or a charmer, or a consulter with familiar spirits, or a wizard, or a necromancer (one who contacts the dead).
> For all that do these things are an abomination unto the Lord: and because of these abominations the Lord thy God doth drive them out from before thee" (Deuteronomy 18:10-12).

So all the people who involve themselves in séances who think they are speaking to the spirits of their dead loved ones are really speaking to demons who are impersonating them and are, not only being deceived but are in sin. These practices are hated by God, but the reason He does not want you to get involved is, not because He wants to spoil your fun, but to keep you safe.

> "...and I would not that ye should have fellowship with devils.
> Ye cannot drink the cup of the Lord, and the cup of devils; ye cannot be partakers of the Lord's Table and of the table of devils" (1 Corinthians 10:20b, 21).

In the past few decades, there has been an explosion of interest in communicating with the dead, and with other spirits. There has been an ever increasing line up of TV shows with this content and apparitions of the Virgin Mary, where millions across the globe are being deceived. Those who are involved in these kinds of practices don't understand (or are intentionally ignoring) the great spiritual risks they are taking.

Unbeknownst to many, our God has supplied us with a Manufacturer's Handbook, the Bible but if you have not read the Bible, there is no way for you to know these things. That is the position I was in.

Channeling Spirits with Automatic Writing

Soon I was reading cards, and channeling spirits to receive automatic writing. I was doing all this in an attempt to communicate with my mother's spirit and ultimately get to know God. Every night at 2:00 o'clock in the morning I would go into a trance and a demon would come and pretend to be a "good spirit" and take hold of my hand. I would receive volumes of automatic writing in this way. I have since learned that many of the books in the occult and new age sections of libraries were written by demons by way of automatic writing.

In these volumes of this automatic writing the spirits gave me an entire counterfeit rapture scenario and told me that the "chosen ones" were going to escape the calamities coming on the earth. Earth was going to tilt on its axis causing great catastrophic events to occur. The poles would shift and there would be meteors hitting the earth. Certain people would be chosen to leave earth before that happened, however, and I happened to be one of the chosen ones.

Ah ha! I always knew I had been *chosen* now it was beginning to make sense. I was chosen to escape the disastrous things that were to come. Not only that, but I had also been chosen to help gather all the other people who had been chosen as well. The false plan that was given to me was that we would go to a remote place in Canada, which was yet to be revealed, and there, engineers would build a space ship, according to given specifications and when the time was right, we would be taken up in a whirlwind and go to Mars escaping the earth's devastation. (If the devil has gone to the trouble of creating a counterfeit catching away, then you know there is going to be a real one, a real gathering and catching away of God's chosen ones going, not to Mars, but to heaven to be with Him. Christians call this real coming event "The Rapture of the Church."

Wait, just a minute, I would write back to these spirits, Mars is uninhabitable. Oh no, there is life under the surface they would tell me. Now all this sounds crazy. But you know what---recently this is what scientists are telling us that in the year 2012 catastrophic things are going to begin happening on the earth. There will be a strange alignment of planets that will cause this. Meteors will hit and cause the earth to tilt on its axis. This tilting of the earth's axis will result in catastrophic weather patterns and a shift in the poles. The North Pole will be at the South Pole. This has happened before and has happened quickly. Do you remember learning about those Mastodons encapsulated in ice with food still in their stomachs? There will be solar storms that will cause the earth's temperature to rise to life threatening levels. Oh, and they are also saying that there is life beneath the surface of Mars. There have actually been documentaries in the last few years on television. The History channel and several other channels have been featuring this information. A few years ago they had an entire week called Armageddon week. The world knows that the wheels are coming off. But they don't know what to do about it. It used to be the Church preaching gloom and doom to the world, but when the Church preaches, there is hope with a way out. Now the world is preaching the gloom and doom with no way out. Think of the fear this is creating in people. Let us pray that the fear will bring those in the world to their knees.

The spirits I was communicating with were like people without bodies. Mainly in the western world today even Christians, do not want to see the reality of the realm of the devil. It has been severely watered down. I can tell you, however, that the spirits I was communicating with were, indeed, people without bodies. Very intelligent people without bodies just looking for a body to inhabit so they could carry out their evil, nefarious deeds. They were pretending to be my dead relatives with the promise of getting me in touch with my mother and ultimately with God. The devil's only power over us is deception and he does a good job of deceiving many by counterfeiting the Lord. He was counterfeiting the Holy Spirit telling me that by being patient and doing what he said, I would eventually reach God. There's only one way to get into communication with God, and that is the New Birth.

Lions, and Tigers, and Bears, Oh My!

These spirits began ruthlessly attacking me. They explained the attacks by telling me that there were good spirits and bad spirits and that I had to get through the bad ones first, then I would contact the good ones and go on to God. It was something like the Wizard of Oz – Dorothy had encountered lions, tigers, and bears on her way to the emerald throne. Yeh right! What a counterfeit! It's not the Wizard of Oz whose throne is emerald, but God's.

REDEEMING HARD TIME AND HARD TIMES

"And He that sat was to look upon like a jasper and a sardine stone: and there was a rainbow round about the throne, in sight like unto an emerald" (Revelation 4:3).

Very strange things were beginning to happen to me. Things in our apartment would move around. I would see visions of things that were not there to anyone else and hear things that no one else could hear. I would go into rages that caused my kids and their friends to begin to be terrified of me. Everyone thought I was going crazy and for all intents and purposes I WAS.

These "bad" spirits I was in contact with would give me heart attack symptoms and then at other times suddenly all the strength would drain out of me and I would be so weak I could hardly stand. I would be taken across the street to the hospital thinking I was dying. When my strength would suddenly return I would bolt out of the emergency room back out on the street. I am sure the doctors thought I was one of the crazy homeless souls who roamed the streets in that area.

I was being hurt spiritually, emotionally, and physically. If I did not do the crazy things the demons told me to do they would attack. I remember thinking that the mental hospitals were full of people who were not really crazy but rather possessed by these things. At one point I was told by these voices that everything green in my apartment was cursed and I had to get it out, the problem was that just about everything in the apartment was green. Green was my favorite color. When my kids came home from school and saw what I was doing, they knew for sure I was going insane. They had become so convinced I would die as a result of all that was happening to me that they were beginning to make plans for their future without me. My daughter and her boyfriend planned to marry and take care of the boys, therefore keeping the family together.

One night I was washing my hair, when the voices told me to get out of the apartment. Clad in my bathrobe, with a towel wrapped around my wet head I ran out into the street and hitch hiked a ride downtown to a Catholic church where I was compelled to kneel down before the statue of Mary. The statue talked to me and told me I was going to be the next Virgin Mary. A priest approached me asking if he could help me in any way. I reached out my hand to his and I had pills in it. Of course he was sure I was just another junkie off the street. At that, I ran out of the church. I never did figure out where those pills came from and I have no memory of how I got back home that night. These are only a few examples of my behavior at this time. I was pretty far gone. But, you know, you are never too far gone for Jesus to come and rescue you.

CHAPTER 5

Finding God

Where Was He in All This?

WHAT BEGAN TO be a search for my dead mother was turning into a search for the living God. I thought that I was doing all the supernatural stuff in service to Him but I was beginning to realize that I had been deceived. My guess is that I was finally realizing that I had not contacted God, but rather had contacted something very evil, so now, I had to find God. I instinctively knew that He was the only way out of this mess. But where was God, how do you find Him? Can He indeed be found? These were some of the questions in my mind. I knew He existed, but where was He? I knew He had saved my life a few times when I thought I only had seconds to live, and if I could find the devil, I certainly should be able to find God. What I did not realize was that God wasn't lost, I was.

God Had Saved My Life Before

God had saved my life on a few occasions before this was all happening. It seemed reasonable to me that if He saved my life before, He could do it again. It had been only a few years before when the devil took some swipes at my life. But ironically just as the devil was trying his best to keep me for himself, God was using it all to draw me to Him and those near death experiences caused me to have faith that God could save me yet again.

One of those near death swipes at my life came one spring day. I was on a Donzi, a very high performance race boat, in a race going about 60 miles an hour on Lake Erie. It was at the beginning of May when the water was still very cold. The boat hit a wave, the steering wheel broke, the kill switch was too long and the driver rolled into the back seat instead of getting thrown out. I, on the other hand, did get thrown out. I held on and got battered against the hull of the boat until I was violently wrenched free. A strong voice, this time, the HOLY Spirit, I'm sure, said to me as I began skimming across the surface of the water, "Whatever you do, don't lose consciousness." As if taking an order from a Senior Officer, I said, yes Sir. Had I lost consciousness, I would have surely sunk to the bottom of that cold murky water that day and drowned. My body may never have been found. I don't know how I knew it, but I knew that there was an angel holding me up on the surface of the water and helping me to tread water. The miracle is that I can't tread water, I never could and I had no life jacket on and was badly hurt. Another boater in the race saw what had happened, turned around and pulled me out of the water.

At the hospital the doctors were sure I had many broken bones. After they looked at the x-rays, however, they were amazed when they discovered that I didn't have a broken bone in my body. My entire side was so bruised that it was navy blue for weeks, and my ankle was sore and swollen for some time but miraculously I had no broken bones. There was no doubt in my mind that it was God who saved me that day.

Still another time the devil tried to take my life was in a restaurant at a Junior Chamber of Commerce dinner when suddenly a piece of steak became lodged in my throat. All I could do was stand up and grab my throat. I couldn't talk, I couldn't breathe. The thought that ran through my mind was that Ethel Kennedy's sister had recently died that way in a restaurant and I was going to die the same way. I knew I had only moments to live, when suddenly I was wrenched from my chair, bent over a railing by a large man who did the Heimlich maneuver on me and my life was saved. Unbeknownst to me I just happened to be sitting next to the Fire Chief of that community and of course he knew just what to do. I was convinced the devil was trying to kill me but God would not allow it, I just didn't know yet what it all meant.

Entertaining Angels Unawares

"Be not forgetful to entertain strangers: for thereby some have entertained angels unawares" (Hebrews 13:2).

I had begun receiving correspondence lessons in Wicca and was shocked to read that they were denying Jesus was the incarnate God. They named several others throughout history who could have been, but not Jesus. They were quoting Scripture and it really got me interested in knowing more about Jesus. The lessons were also teaching about Pontius Pilate. I remembered learning something about him from my childhood Catholic catechism lessons and began to wonder why I had been reading everything else but the Bible so I went to the bookstore to find one. Once again the devil drew me in his direction because what I found instead was the Anton La Vey satanic bible. As I began to read its hedonistic philosophies I got a phone call from a young man who said he and I had a mutual friend. He never told me who that friend was. In looking back I have often wondered if it was Jesus. He proceeded to tell me that everything I needed to know was in the Bible. I kept quoting the satanic verses to him and pretty much told him he was a fool.

I couldn't figure him out. Guys usually wanted to date me, but he just wanted to tell me about God and that all I needed to know was in the Bible. He said it several times. He wanted to meet me so I told him what club I would be working in that night and sure enough, he showed up. He and I sat at the bar where he drank a coke and kept telling me all I needed to know was in the Bible. A few years later after I was already saved I heard that someone picked up a hitch hiker who was an angel; I told God that I would like to meet an angel. To my complete surprise, He said to me, "You did" and He took my mind back to that young man who kept telling me that everything I needed to know was in the Bible.

Voices in My Head

I started backing off the channeling and automatic writing in an attempt to get to some form of normalcy once again and was functioning fairly well when a friend, who was also interested in witchcraft, asked me one day if I wanted to go to a séance. Of course I did, it was all so exciting. This séance was being held at the home of a woman who called herself a witch. She lived in a farm house where there was a large round table that stood in the middle of a huge country kitchen. After we were finished speaking to the spirits, and just sitting there having coffee, I suddenly

PART 1: WHAT IS CHRISTIANITY ANYWAY?

got viciously attacked in the small of my back. The force attacking me caused a blood curdling scream to emanate from me. The force attacking me was so powerful that it threw everyone who was sitting at the big round table backward off their chairs into the corners of the room.

After that night, the voices were not only on the outside or in writing form; they were now in my head. Paranoid fear overwhelmed me and was with me wherever I would go. When you are afraid of something, generally you can remove yourself from the source of the fear but it is impossible to remove yourself from voices in your head. Did you see that Madea play where Tyler Perry said he had 27 people livin' up there in his head? Well, that is how I was my friends. Crazy!

Although I had gotten to the point where I was functioning rather well in between the demonic attacks, this was now a turning point. This is when the attacks became so severe that there were no "in between" attacks any more, they were constant. They were now inside my body. I had become possessed. I already had to cut down to working part time but now could no longer function at a job and had to quit working entirely.

Some people who hear voices in their heads think they are from God. More than once we have heard stories in the news about individuals who carried out evil, including murder, because they were obeying voices they thought were from God. In looking back, I am grateful that I didn't think for one minute that the voices I was hearing were God. I knew better than that. I knew that these "people without bodies" were evil. At this point in time I had considered myself to be a Wiccan, a good witch. Make no mistake about it, there is no such thing as a "good witch." Wiccans didn't believe in the devil so it was all very confusing. They believed in good spirits and bad spirits, but not demons. However, I was now beginning to get the picture, the truth...maybe the spirits who were attacking me really were devils after all.

I was still on drugs, but they had become the least of my problems, or so I thought. Actually drugs and witchcraft are two sides of the same coin. Revelation 18:23 teaches that the nations in the last days will be deceived by their sorceries. The Greek word there is *pharmakeia*. – Sound familiar – pharmacy – pharmaceuticals – drugs. Drug abuse, according to the Bible equates to sorcery. No one can deny that in these last days, drug abuse and the deception that goes along with it is pandemic. I believe that the spirit over America today is pharmakeia, and that includes legal drugs as well. Think about it, never before have you seen so many commercials on television for drugs or so many drug store pharmacies thriving even in a poor economy. People are taking drugs for everything under the sun these days and the drug companies keep coming up with more.

"And the light of a candle shall shine no more at all in thee (The end time Babylon); and the voice of the bridegroom and of the bride shall be heard no more at all in thee: for thy merchants were the great men of the earth; for by thy sorceries (pharmakeia) were all nations deceived" (Revelation 18:23).

I think you would all agree that drug addiction is the biggest source of deception in the world today, and it is sure to get worse in the final days.

Message Service; Prayer Requests

At one point I went to a lady who called herself a Metaphysician, a new age practitioner. She instructed me to recite the

91st Psalm whenever I was feeling oppressed or under attack. Sometimes even non-Christians have some wisdom. I took her advice and finally cracked a Bible.

The 91st Psalm, although not magic, like the Metaphysical lady seemed to think it was, helped me tremendously. First of all, it got me into the Bible, and secondly, it was finally the Word of Almighty God going into my spirit. It is a powerful passage of Scripture that you too can gain great peace from in your times of oppression.

"He that dwelleth in the secret place of the Most High shall abide under the shadow of the Almighty.

I will say of the Lord, He is my refuge and my fortress: my God; in Him will I trust.

Surely He shall deliver thee from the snare of the fowler, and from the noisesome pestilence

He shall cover thee with His feathers, and under His wings shalt thou trust; His truth shall be thy shield and buckler.

Thou shalt not be afraid for the terror by night; nor for the arrow that flieth by day;

Nor for the pestilence that walketh in darkness; nor for the destruction that wasteth at noonday.

A thousand shall fall at thy side, and ten thousand at thy right hand; but it shall not come nigh thee.

Only with thine eyes shalt thou behold and see the reward of the wicked.

For He shall give His angels charge over thee to keep thee in all thy ways.

They shall bear thee up in their hands, lest thou dash thy foot against a stone.

Thou shalt tread upon the lion and adder; the young lion and the dragon shalt thou trample under feet.

Because he hath set his love upon me, therefore will I deliver him: I will set him on high, because he hath known My Name.

He shall call upon me, and I will answer him; I will be with him in trouble; I will deliver him, and honor him.

With long life will I satisfy him, and show him my salvation" (Psalm 91).

I began thinking that perhaps going to church would help and not knowing what church to go to and as dumb as it may seem, I rationalized that if you have trouble with spirits, you go to a spiritualist church, right? WRONG! I began to attend spiritualist churches where their services were called "message services." Someone would get up in front of the congregation and give messages he or she would receive from spirits. It was counterfeit prophecy. I would attend many of these meetings and ask for help to get these "bad" spirits off of me. After every attempt had failed, even they became afraid of me and would no longer allow me to attend their meetings. I was in such serious condition by this time and convinced that if I did not find help soon surely it would lead to my death. So, in desperation I kept looking for other spiritualists. I found my way to the devil, but how could I find my way to God?

Bea Rake

Spiritualists would advertise the locations of their "message services" with cryptic personal ads so I continued to search the ads in the newspapers. When I found an ad that read, *message service – prayer requests*. I called the telephone number and left a message about what I had been

PART 1: WHAT IS CHRISTIANITY ANYWAY?

experiencing and that I desperately needed prayer. I didn't expect anyone to call me back, but three days later a precious lady named Bea Rake called me. She wasn't a spiritualist, the "message service" in the ad meant you could leave a message and someone would pray for you. Well, it turned out that she was the wife of Don Rake, the president of an organization called the Full Gospel Business Men's Fellowship International, the ministry sponsoring the advertisement. She proceeded to tell me that she had been praying and fasting for me for three days.

This brave lady told me about Jesus and that I needed to ask Him to forgive me and to come into my life. Curiously, she kept saying things during the conversation like, *"Now that I know God...before I knew God..."* I wondered why she knew God and I didn't after all I had been doing for Him and searching for Him. I thought I was telling fortunes for God, go figure. She asked me if I had a Bible – my husband had left his old Sunday school Bible behind so I went and got it. She told me to look up a Scripture. I was shocked at what it said.

"Thou shalt not suffer a witch to live" (Exodus 22:18).

No wonder I was dying, I thought – all along I assumed that witchcraft was the highest and deepest you could go with God and now I learned it is, instead, an abomination to God. That night, even though my thought was that I had transcended that Sunday School Jesus stuff, I sobbed and prayed, "Jesus, I am so confused I don't even know who you are anymore, but if you are real, forgive me and come into my life and help me clean up this mess I have made."

Connecting the Dots

After the night when I cried myself to sleep and reached out to God, I didn't expect anything to happen. After all, it had only been 18 months since I cried out to God to not let my mother die, and she died anyway. He didn't seem to hear me then, why should I think He would hear me now? What I didn't realize was that this time I really meant it from my heart. So a few days later, even though I still wasn't connecting the dots and realizing that God was at work in my life, I asked a friend if he would stay over the weekend and watch the kids because I wanted to crash, and get off the drugs cold turkey. Although I had never been addicted to hard drugs, heroin, cocaine, or LSD, I was addicted to and could not get through a day without amphetamines. Of course, he thought I was crazy but agreed to do it anyway. I slept a lot all that weekend and amazingly, after trying many times before unsuccessfully to quit the drugs, I was home free after 13 years of addiction. No withdrawals and no more pills!

I was still smoking four packs of cigarettes a day, however, yes four packs! I would smoke three during the day and because I was working half the night in the clubs, I would smoke another pack there and as a result was having severe breathing problems. Then, I began to experience terrible chest pains as well. I went to see a doctor at a nearby clinic and when he said I needed to go to the hospital for tests, suddenly the fear of death swept over me like an evil black cloud.

Bea Rake, the lady who had ministered to me on the phone a few weeks before had given me her telephone number and I had put it in my wallet. I immediately went out into the lobby of the clinic and called her. I told her I was desperate and would do anything and I meant it! "PRAISE THE LORD," she squealed. "There just happens to be a miracle healing service tonight." Wow, this lady is whacked, I said to myself. But aware that she had something I wanted, I agreed to meet her and attend this service. I hadn't been able to eat and my weight had gone down to 100 pounds. I had not slept but a few hours in several weeks and was completely exhausted. I knew that if God would not help me that night, I would surely die.

Jesus is Real!

Bea and I arranged to meet and she took me to the church where this miracle healing service was being held. Once inside this awesome cathedral like church building and seated in the balcony I immediately heard angels singing in tongues along with the congregation. I had sung in choirs and was fully aware that it took a considerable amount of effort to achieve harmony, but although everyone in the church, and the angels were singing different songs, they all sounded heavenly and they were all in one accord. I could see the angels. They were so close together on the ceiling of that church that they actually blocked some of the light. Hundreds of people in the congregation sang, "Jesus is Real", and "He Touched Me."

Suddenly, without even thinking about it, my hands went up into the air and with tears streaming down my face, and my eyes closed, I saw a vision of Jesus. He was standing right there in front of me and He took hold of my hands. I did not see His face, but as He held my hands I saw that He had robes on. I was amazed that He really did have robes on just like the pictures I had seen of Him from the time I was a child. Although the Bible says that He is seated on the right hand of the Father, Jesus actually stood that night to receive this wretched sinner into His Kingdom.

I finally found God. I remember thinking that even though everyone in my life had deserted me; the very Creator of the universe loved me and invited me to belong to Him. I knew that everything was going to be alright. He spoke many words to me in an instant of time. He told me that I would be going through what would seem like a mine field in a war zone but if I held onto His hand, He knew the way through that mine field and that war zone and would lead me through to the other side and on to victory. I have since learned that sometimes the only way out IS through.

Jesus is Alive!

Much to my surprise I saw that down at the altar the older couple, Charles and Frances Hunter, who were conducting the service were actually casting out devils and people were getting healed and set free. They were collecting cigarettes in shopping bags and pointing out that if you belong to God then you are the temple of the Holy Spirit and the Holy Spirit doesn't smoke. I had huffed and puffed all the way there. I desperately wanted to be free of those nasty cigarettes because they had become such a terrible addiction and bondage in my life. So, although we were way up in the balcony, far away from the people collecting the packs of cigarettes from the congregation down below, I made a decision in my heart to put my cigarettes into one of those bags too and prayed that God would help me give them up for good. Well, I went for three days after that without one and on the fourth day picked them up again.

For the next three days, every time I would put a cigarette

to my mouth and light it, a voice in my heart, not my head, would say to me, "You have the power inside of you now not to do that." Then, one day I just threw the cigarettes and lighter out of my car window and never wanted another one again. I was free!

I knew I had found God in that church. When I realized that they were casting out devils I went down to the altar area and asked for prayer. I told the lady that I was being tormented by demons. Yes, by this time I knew they, indeed, were demons. She wasn't afraid of me, and didn't think I was crazy like the spiritualists did, she simply laid hands on my head and said, "Devil, in the Name of Jesus, get out." I slept the night after the church service for the first time in weeks. To keep the demons away I kept saying to myself, "Jesus is real." "Jesus is alive." I had never considered that He was not only real, but alive. He was alive, not dead, like the spirits I had contacted.

Life Was Never To Be the Same Again

The next night I took my children to that service and they too got gloriously saved. After having such a powerful encounter with the living God it was easy for me to make the decision to lay everything down that was not of God. A week later, however, after that wonderful service, the demons began to come back with a vengeance and harass me again. My new friend Bea told me I needed deliverance. I told her I didn't know what it was but whatever it was, I wanted it. I had grown to trust her and called her often for advice.

I may not have started out so great but I was determined to finish well. Because of Jesus we all have the opportunity to finish well. Just like I did, you too can have another chance at life. This is only the beginning for you but you will find that the challenges you face after you leave here will be greater than the challenges you faced inside. Remember what Paul tells us in Philippians 3:13 and 14 not to look back in such a way that it will keep you in bondage to the past. Your past is your past. You have a wonderful future to look forward to.

"But now, after that ye have known God, or rather are known of God, how turn ye again to the weak and beggarly elements, whereunto ye desire again to be in bondage?" (Galatians 4:9).

Taking the time to tell you where I was just before and after I became wonderfully saved and filled with the Holy Spirit of God is important. It is important in that I want you to get a picture of where Jesus has brought me from to where I am today, from high school drop out to six college degrees, two of which are doctorates I also have a wonderful, life, filled with children, grandchildren, and great grandchildren. It is my desire that you get a glimpse of where God can take you in your life as well. But don't sit on the fence and be a double-minded Christian. Double-minded Christians are those who have just enough of the world in them to be miserable in the Lord and just enough of the Lord in them to be miserable in the world. The Word says:

"Submit yourselves therefore unto God, Resist the devil, and he will flee from you. Draw nigh to God, and He will draw nigh to you. Cleanse your hands, ye sinners, and purify your hearts, ye double minded" (James 4:7).

Why Do These Deceptions Work

People who become victims of the kind of deception I

found myself entangled in sometimes *want* to have these experiences in the foolish belief that they are somehow being enlightened, or getting some secret knowledge about the future, the universe, the spirit world or healing powers. Some victims, just like I was, are desperate to believe the experiences are real because they deeply miss a deceased loved one and begin to believe they are actually communicating with them when they are really communicating with devils. Their emotional reaction to the experiences can overwhelm their ability to see the truth about what's really happening, especially if they hear something from their allegedly deceased loved one. This is the state of mind in which I found myself. I began to have doubts, and at first was in a state of denial. I began to suspect that I was dealing with evil entities but they kept telling me that they were harmless and that eventually I would get through to my deceased mother, aunts and uncles. I did not realize that demons can appear as angels of light.

"For such are false apostles, deceitful workers, transforming themselves into the apostles of Christ.
And no marvel; for Satan himself is transformed into an angel of light" (2 Corinthians 11:13, 14).

Why Demons Want to Mislead You?

The simple answer to this question is that demons want to control your life and possess you. For the unsaved person, their goal is to prevent him or her from discovering the truth of the Bible and the free gift of salvation through faith in the Lord Jesus Christ. Satan knows he is doomed to hell and wants to pull as many of us as possible right along with him. The loss of my mother is what started it all. It was reminding me of my own mortality and that I needed God. The loss of a loved one should be a reminder to all of us of our own mortality. It should drive us all into God's loving arms for comfort, and for those who haven't yet accepted Jesus, that is exactly what can happen to you. All these demonic experiences were the very thing that pushed me closer to God. We must be careful that in our times of grief we are not deceived by Satan and lured away from the saving grace of the Lord Jesus Christ.

CHAPTER 6

Victory Takes Time

We Don't Get Messed Up Overnight

WE DIDN'T GET messed up overnight and we can't expect to get well overnight. Becoming more and more like Christ takes time; it is called sanctification. I have told you about my life just before I came to the Lord and how I suffered trauma after trauma, crisis after crisis, and explained that the life I was leading, well, let's just say I was not exactly a girl scout. But the main reason I got into so much danger is because I did not have knowledge of the Word of God in me. You see, when you have knowledge of the truth. THAT is what will give you the victory. It is the truth that will set you free and keep you free.

"My people are destroyed for lack of knowledge" (Hosea 4:6a).

God is talking about HIS people here. You don't find anywhere in Scripture any other way that God's people can be destroyed, except for lack of knowledge. If I would have known what the Word of God teaches, I would not have gotten into such deep deception and delusion. If YOU would have known... or maybe you did know but chose to ignore it or just simply didn't believe it. The Bible really is the Manufacturer's Handbook for living.

Strange, isn't it how we just don't think about what the consequences could be when we are engaged in sinful behavior? Consequences are not being taught these days in homes, at school or even in church. It is illegal to spank your kids and teachers do not dare to discipline unruly students so that young people today do not have any concept of cause and effect. It is the same in the realm of the spiritual. Sin and its consequences are not being preached like they should be in the church so that when believers get into spiritual trouble, they don't know how to get out or who to turn to for help. Knowing your enemy is vital. Those of you who were in the armed forces know that one of the first things you are taught about is the enemy you will be facing. One of the most basic principles of warfare is to know your enemy and never underestimate him. If you don't understand the enemy's situation you are going to get clobbered!

That is the way it is in spiritual warfare. If you don't have a basic understanding of what you are fighting against you will find yourself in deep trouble with no apparent way out. That is what happened to me, I found myself in a deep, dark place with no knowledge of how to escape.

Deception

My darkness was witchcraft, but yours may be something else. No matter what it is that you are dealing with, drug abuse, addiction, criminal activity, alcoholism, violent behavior,

PART 1: WHAT IS CHRISTIANITY ANYWAY?

incarceration, the answer is the same, Jesus! Your darkness may not be as sinister as witchcraft and it may be worse, but it all involves deception. Deception is the devil's only weapon against you and if you don't know the Truth which is Jesus, the devil will have the upper hand in your life and you will fall for his lies every time.

No matter what your sin, it is all deception. I cited a Scripture in Revelation 18:23 in an earlier chapter regarding deception. The Greek word used there for magic spells and poisonous charms is pharmakeia. It is obvious that our word pharmaceutical is derived from that root Greek word. Of course, it is not referring here to medications that are used to help make you well. Rather it is making reference to the kinds of drugs that are abused and those that produce an altered state of consciousness. These kinds of drugs were the ones used in ancient times for magic spells and witchcraft and in some circles, are still used this way today. The book of Revelation describes scenarios of this kind of deception that is taking place in these, the very last of days.

If you have fallen away, whatever it was that may have caused you to fall away from God, there is only one way back and that is Jesus. Of course it starts with being born-again, but you see, that is only the beginning. As I mentioned in chapter 1, your spirit gets saved immediately but getting free in your soul, which is comprised of your mind and emotions, doesn't all happen overnight and sometimes isn't an easy road to travel. But I can assure you, it IS worth it. The Apostle Paul knew that and said:

"Wherefore, my beloved, as ye have always obeyed, not as in my presence only, but now much more in my absence, work out your own salvation with fear and trembling.

For it is God which worketh in you both to will and to do of His good pleasure" (Philippians 2:12-13).

Ruth & Del Carlton

For about one week after my glorious encounter with the Lord Jesus Christ in that miracle healing service I began to experience demonic attacks once again. My new friend and sister in the Lord, Bea told me I probably needed deliverance. I had never even heard the term and told her, "Whatever that is, I want it!" She proceeded to tell me about a couple who had a deliverance ministry.

I called and made an appointment with a lady named Ruth and arrived at her home a few days later. As she began to counsel me the one thing that really touched my heart was how she was showing me so much love. She didn't even know me but in spite of all the terrible things I was telling her about myself, things I had never told another person before in my life, she calmly acted as though she still loved me. It was so unusual because all my life, I had known condemnation, criticism, judgment and rejection, yet I felt so very comfortable here with her. She explained to me that renouncing would take the hurt out of the memories, curses, circumstances and sins which had all opened doors and invited Satan into my life. Then, once the renouncing took away Satan's legal ground, it would be much easier to cast him out.

"Therefore, seeing we have this ministry, as we have received mercy, we faint not.
But have renounced the hidden things of dishonesty, not walking in craftiness, nor handling the Word of God deceitfully, but by manifestation of the truth commending ourselves

PART 1: WHAT IS CHRISTIANITY ANYWAY?

to every man's conscience in the sight of God" (2 Corinthians 4:1,2).

For hours Ruth questioned me; taking notes on sins I had committed from childhood and gave me Scriptures to read pertaining to each sin. She said that the Word of God was like a powerful sword that could actually work to separate the spirits from me and how every demon has to manifest himself the sight of God.

"For the Word of God is quick and powerful, and sharper than any two-edged sword, piercing even to the dividing asunder of soul and spirit, and of the joints and marrow, and is a discerner of the thoughts and intents of the heart.
Neither is there any creature that is not manifest in His sight: but all things are naked and open unto the eyes of Him with whom we have to do" (Hebrews 4:12, 13).

When Ruth's husband, Del, came home, I took one look at him and said, "I know you!" I recognized him as the man I stood next to at the miracle healing service, and the same man who prayed for me at the Christian dinner that Bea took me to! All these coincidences made me feel as though God was surely in this. I felt the same kind of warmth and love from Del as I did from his wife Ruth. Together they counseled me and prayed for me for seven straight hours. No stranger ever cares that much for a person but with the love of Jesus, they cared that much for me.

I was amazed at how wonderful it felt to confess and even more amazed to learn that the Bible was God's instruction manual for humans; the Manufacturer's Handbook no less. Together they cast many spirits out of me that night and when we were finished, I asked the Lord for a heavenly language and He gave one to me.

"And these signs shall follow them that believe; in My Name shall they cast out devils, they shall speak with new tongues" (Mark 16:17).

I sang in the spirit all the way home. I had never felt so much peace before. I had begun to love and be loved, forgive and be forgiven, breaking the powerful patterns of rejection and rebellion that had been so prevalent in my life. Ruth also explained to me that I should read my Bible every day, and that I would be sanctified and made holy through it and that my mind would be renewed and cleansed with the washing of the water of the Word.

That He might sanctify and cleanse it (the church, that's us) *with the washing of water by the Word that He might present it to Himself a glorious church, not having spot or wrinkle or any such thing, but that it should be holy and without blemish" (Ephesians 5:26)*

Ruth and Del instructed me that now that I had confessed my sins, and gotten evil spirits cast out, I was to get rid of all my occult objects so that I could stay free.

"And many that believed came, and confessed, and showed their deeds.
Many of them also which used curious arts brought their books together, and burned them before all men: and they counted the price of them, and found it fifty thousand pieces of silver.

So mightily grew the Word of God and prevailed" (Acts 19:18-20).

When War Has Been Declared, You Can't Retreat

When an army goes to war, there is no turning back until the battle has been won. We knew there was only one way to go and that was forward, toward the things of God. When the Spirit of the Lord began to show us to get rid of the things we were in possession of that were not of God, we obeyed. You can't be concerned about how much something is worth; you can't put a price on peace. I knew the Lord was in this so I asked Him to show me what to get rid of.

I had been an artist and had done some beautiful oils, among them a self portrait that for years my children were terrified of. They would cover it with towels when I wasn't home because its eyes would follow them around the room. Ruth told me that, depending on the spiritual condition of the artist, spirits could live in pictures and objects of art. So out it went with an entire book of poetry I had written that was filled with gloom, doom, depression, and death. Out went zodiac jewelry, mementos, occult children's games, books and literature, psychedelic posters, strobe lights, record albums, and tapes, and half my wardrobe that was not fit for a Christian woman to be wearing. There was an incinerator door right outside our apartment so into the fire they went. The more I would burn, the more the Holy Spirit would show me to burn. After I was finished, our apartment seemed to get shades lighter and brighter and so much more pleasant. From that time on the children and I would often go into every room and commanded any spirit that was still there to leave in the Name of Jesus.

Walking in the Miraculous

Although we were fighting in a spiritual war against the devil, we were simultaneously beginning to walk in the miraculous. The Lord was showing us that even having the ability to cast out a devil is a miracle. By this time we were devouring the Word, going to many Christian activities for fellowship, studying and being counseled.

We sought out discipleship and placed ourselves under the loving care of Christians. The deliverance ministry my friend Bea led us to was called Freedom House. There was a service there every week which we attended faithfully. We were learning how to pray to God and against the enemy and learning the strategies with which to do battle against Satan. I was still having waves of attacks, however, and physical manifestations in my body. Ruth assured me that they would eventually leave and prayed with me often.

As hard as I tried not to hear anything from the enemy, I knew that he was going to hurt my children if I continued to fight against him. I had a decision to make, either I listened to him or listened to and trusted God. I chose to put my trust in God. My children did get attacked. My older son, Bobby, would go into violent, uncontrolled rages. When he would give in to the temptations of smoking marijuana, sniffing glue, and drinking wine, we would bind those spirits and cast them out of him. He would get terribly harassed at night and spirits would speak to him in audible voices terrifying him with threats of murder. We came against these spirits of harassment, intoxication and murder and he was set free. Thank God, my youngest son, Scotty, did not seem to be as affected as the rest of us.

My daughter Cherie would also be harassed by audible voices, and spirits would try to throw her down the stairs. It seemed at times we were fighting a losing battle. Her boyfriend, Norby, who would eventually become her husband, was also getting harassed. Before we would get through one encounter, another skirmish would break out somewhere else. Aside from all the warfare, we were also constantly battling depression and discouragement. But, through it all, Jesus was ever so present in our lives. He was performing miracles and wonders daily. He would speak in many ways, assuring us that He would never leave us or forsake us and we continued to praise the Lord for everything. We knew that if God had gotten us this far, He would not let us down but we couldn't back away and retreat

Covered By the Blood of Jesus

We were learning that Jesus had covered our sin with His blood so that Satan no longer had a right to stay. Most think that sin is black but the Bible refers to sin as being scarlet. When the red blood of Jesus is applied to our red sin it covers our red sin and He sees us as sinless.

"Come now, and let us reason together, saith the Lord: though your sins be as scarlet, they shall be as white as snow; though they be red like crimson, they shall be as wool" (Isaiah 1:18).

So, although I would get attacked, I now understood that Satan had to leave. After the passing of time the waves of attacks were getting weaker and weaker and less frequent, especially during the days. The paranoid fear was leaving little by little but the nights were difficult. My kids would pray me through so I could sleep. I would battle with sexual assaults from incubus spirits (sexual spirits who attack during your sleep) and mental harassment all night, every night. I would get held down and paralyzed in my sleep and felt as thought I would die. I learned that my spirit didn't sleep and that I could combat the devil with the Blood of Jesus even in my sleep and he would have to leave.

It didn't take me long to discover that very few Christians knew much about deliverance. Well meaning people, some of them pastors, would insist that because I was a Christian, what was happening to me couldn't possibly be happening to me. Sometimes I would get so discouraged and wonder when it would all end. I would look at my bed and in faith say, "Someday, I am going to be able to sleep without being tormented."

I had been faithfully sitting under the discipleship and spiritual warfare teachings of Ruth and Del; growing, getting grounded in the Word and building a strong foundation. Ruth instructed me to make lists of the things that were going on in my life that were not normal. In making my first list, I would no sooner get it together and I would get viciously attacked in my mind and body once again until I destroyed the list. "That is just what the devil wanted you to do." Ruth explained. So, I bound Satan, toughed it out, and made the list again. Within a few weeks I was back in deliverance and determined not to be defeated. I was in it to win it! I was covered by the Blood of Jesus and the devil had to leave.

Who in the World Am I?

I discovered that I had several layers of schizophrenic personalities that were coming off in layers something like peeling an onion. After we got through with one list and removed a layer, several weeks later the Lord would give me another list and off would come another layer. God showed me that He could not set me free all at once because I needed time for my true personality to ascend and grow strong as the demon powers were broken. With each layer, I had to deal with the flesh and stand against Satan to retain the deliverance. My true personality had been submerged for so long in a sea of demonic activity that I did not know who I really was. I had to come to grips with a new me and a new normal every time but I was coming to know the true me as my own personality grew strong and emerged. I had to walk out of agreement with each layer of my false personality. In the Old Testament book of Amos it tells us:

"Can two walk together, except they be agreed?" (Amos 3:3).

I was no longer in agreement with sin and Satan so now I had to go back into my childhood to when I was having psychic experiences and break those witchcraft curses from my grandmother and great grandmother. As I recalled sins, bad memories, hurts, disappointments, rejections, guilt, and other circumstances that opened doors to the enemy I made more lists. Rather than think of this process as going back and unnecessarily dredging up the past, I thought of it as drilling down to get the infection out. You can't cure cancer by putting a bandage on it; you have to cut it out and you can't get rid of a demon unless you cast it out. Every few weeks Ruth and I would declare war on these things. I would go down new lists, renouncing and casting out devils. For the next few years, we went over my entire life with this process. I was walking out of agreement with my past.

Having the attitude that the devil made me do it never occurred to me. I was taking full responsibility for my actions. I was relieved, however, to realize that I had a lot of help from the devil in doing the things I did. I was learning to *own* my faults, stop blaming others, and realize the devil's involvement in my life at the same time. For the first time in my life I didn't feel like I was a bad person but that I had done bad things and for the first time I was able to separate me from the sin. I wasn't a drug addict - that was what I did, not who I was. I knew who I was now, a child of the Living God. I knew that Jesus loved me but hated the sin, and now I could love me too and hate the sin. I was so relieved that I didn't *have* to sin any more. I didn't *have* to smoke, I didn't *have* to drink, I didn't *have* to work in bars anymore, I didn't *have* to be addicted to drugs, I didn't *have* to use foul language anymore, I didn't *have* to feel like a bad person any more. Praise God!

God was showing me that when we refer to addiction, alcoholism, mental illness, etc., as incurable diseases, there isn't much hope, but when you call them demonic and get deliverance from them and cast them out, now *that* gives you hope! You no longer have to be "a recovering alcoholic." When you are delivered you can be a former one!

As my growth in the Lord and my deliverance progressed I would discover that hurts didn't hurt anymore; disappointments were replaced with divine appointments, and resentment was replaced with love and forgiveness. Sometimes there would be months between deliverance sessions but it just seemed to work out that way and it gave me time to come to grips with another component of my new personality. I learned that the Lord was even in control of the timing because my deliverance had to work in balance with the development of my true self. It could not be rushed because until I was strong in my new self, there would be nothing for me to fall back on.

If every demon would have been cast out of me at once, I would have been totally lost in a sea of confusion and could have had a breakdown; identity with my real self required time and patience. Sometimes I would see myself in the mirror and think that I did not know the person I saw there. These were difficult times of learning to cope with the new areas of me because *me* was constantly changing. No sooner would I become adjusted to the new me and I'd begin to change again.

Throughout this entire process I never took any medication other than aspirin for a headache, which was frequent and that was all. When I needed to be calmed down from a panic attack, we would pray peace over me and the peace of God would engulf me. When the racing thoughts would harass me, we would pray against mind control and my mind would settle down. Before I knew God I would get into such rages that even my children were afraid of me, but now, gradually the anger was leaving. I will never forget the day I was standing in a very slow line at the grocery store. After quite some time of standing there I suddenly realized that I was not in a rage, I was not even angry! What a victory that was. The rages were gone and I never experienced them again. I was gradually being introduced to the real me, the person God had intended me to be all along.

No Victory Without a Battle

It was a long, hard battle because when you are as tangled

in Satan's web of witchcraft, insanity, and deception as I was, he does not let go of you very easily. But, there can't be a victory without a battle. It took a long time, and it may take a long time for you too.

If you feel as though you need deliverance prayer, ask someone to pray with you. Bind Satan, renounce your sin and ask God to forgive you and keep doing this until you get peace. Keep in mind that it took a long time for you to get into this condition so it may take awhile for you to get free but you will get free.

The Apostle Paul instructs us not to be anxious or worried. The one cure for worry is prayer because it is through prayer that we renew our trust in the Lord's faithfulness. When we call on God from a heart that is sincere the peace of God will flood our troubled soul.

"Be careful (anxious) for nothing; but in everything by prayer and supplication with thanksgiving let your requests be make known unto God.

And the Peace of God, which passeth all understanding, shall keep your hearts and minds through Christ Jesus" (Philippians 4:6, 7).

CHAPTER 7

Promises and Fiery Trials

We Will Have Fiery Trials

ALWAYS REMEMBER THAT what we go through is temporary and God is using every bit of it and someday you will be able to help others who have also fallen victim to Satan's devices. I never thought I would be grateful for what I went through, but if I can bring the message of salvation, hope and deliverance to you, and many others in similar circumstances, it has all been worth it.

"*Beloved, do not think it strange concerning the fiery trial which is to try you, as though some strange thing happened unto you:*
But rejoice, inasmuch as ye are partakers of Christ's sufferings; that, when His glory shall be revealed, ye may be glad also with exceeding joy" (1 Peter 4:12, 13).

"*Therefore we do not lose heart. Even though our outward man is perishing, yet the inward man is being renewed day by day.*

REDEEMING HARD TIME AND HARD TIMES

For our light affliction, which is but for a moment, is working for us a far more exceeding and eternal weight of glory. While we do not look at the things which are seen, but at the things which are not seen.

For the things which are seen are temporary, but the things which are not seen are eternal" (2 Corinthians 4:16-18).

"Grace and peace be multiplied unto you through the knowledge of God and of Jesus our Lord.

According as His divine power hath given unto us all things that pertain to life and godliness, through the knowledge of Him that hath called us to glory and virtue:

Whereby are given unto us exceeding great and precious promises, that by these ye may be partakers of the divine nature, having escaped the corruption that is in the world through lust" (2 Peter 1:2-4).

In reading these Scripture passages you can see that God gives us promises. But most of those promises have embedded in them a time of fulfillment and some conditions that must be met. The time in between the promise and the process is when your true spiritual condition is revealed and how willing you are to be obedient and meet those conditions. This is usually the time when the fiery trials heat up. How do we get from the promise to the manifestation, what is the process? The promises of God give us hope and help us in our walk with Him. Some promises are for the individual, some are for the family, while others are for the church as a whole. I want to address the process that every believer goes through to obtain and fulfill those promises.

In chapter 3 we discussed finishing well in spite of starting off in life on the wrong path and taking a detour and finding yourself on a dangerous journey. God's desire for us it to finish well in life and He addresses that concept in His Word.

"Being confident of this very thing, that He which hath begun a good work in you will complete it until the day of Jesus Christ" (Philippians 1:6).

Sounds like a wonderful promise does it not? But if you read down a few verses to 9 through 11 it tells us what God expects in return… this is the process.

"And this I pray, that your love may abound yet more and more in knowledge and in all judgment:
That ye may approve the things that are excellent, that ye may be sincere and without offense till the day of Christ;
Being filled with the fruits of righteousness, which are by Jesus Christ, unto the glory and praise of God" (Philippians 1:9-11).

The Apostle Paul is telling us that we must be ready to live godly if we want to see the precious promises and miracles manifested in our lives. If we are to receive the promise of the completion of the good work God has begun in us we must abound in (have a lot) of knowledge of the Word. We must be able to recognize excellence and approve of it and we must be sincere and without offence in our lives. We must also be filled with the fruit that a righteous life bears.

The Miracles of Obedience

When it comes to being a Christian, righteousness should be our goal. When we get saved we are given the righteousness of Christ in the spiritual, but then we must make a decision to live in righteousness in our flesh. My children and I made the decision that we would do just that; to live as clean and holy as was possible. We wanted everything that God had for us. We wanted His provision, and more of His miracles, and His promises.

As my deliverance from tormenting spirits was progressing our situation in life was progressing as well. I had stopped working in the nightclubs and got a part-time job as a secretary in an engineering firm that fabricated large buckets in which to scoop up slag, sand, pellets, etc., for mining projects. It was a one girl office and I was often there alone with not much to do but answer the phones so to pass the time I would read some of the engineering magazines that came in the mail. One of them was Skilling's Mining Review. In it was a story about the Hibbing Mine being built up on the Mesabi Range in northern Minnesota. The article reported how the rich iron ore had all been mined out of the ground. Taconite ore remained in the rock but it was very difficult to extrapolate. Engineers, however, had discovered a way to grind the ore out of rock with huge autogenous mills and produce pellets. I was fascinated by the article.

Trusting Welfare or Trusting God

In the quiet moments there at my desk the Lord would speak to my heart about getting off welfare and trusting Him. I struggled with that not quite knowing how I could manage to live on the $65.00 a week I was earning. I finally gave in and called the welfare office and told them what I was making. The procedure was that they would deduct that amount from my welfare check. Well, the next month I received the

PART 1: WHAT IS CHRISTIANITY ANYWAY?

full amount again. I called them again, and the next month I received the same, full amount yet again. This time, as I was on the phone with the welfare department, the Lord spoke to me loud and clear. "I told you to get off of welfare and trust Me, not get it reduced!" Wow! Okay, okay, I thought and I told the person at the welfare office to take me completely off the welfare rolls.

A few days later, the phone at my desk rang and it was Del Carlton. He told me that there was an opening at his engineering firm for which he thought I would qualify. I was to interview the very next day. I discovered that this was the very firm that was mining for Taconite and building the autogenous mills at the Hibbing Mine on the Mesabe Range in northern Minnesota. You can only imagine my surprise and the surprise of the engineers to realize that I knew all about their project. This knowledge caused me to have immediate favor in their sight and they hired me on the spot.

Talk about a miracle! Or, I should say a series of miracles. Wow. Only God could have pulled this one off. I just happened to be in the right place at the right time with the right magazine in front of me with the right article that I just happened to find interesting. "Trust Me!" God said, "Get off welfare and I will take care of you." You see what can happen when you obey God even if what He is asking you to do is something that seems to be impossible? Actually, the things He usually asks you to do are impossible with man, but not with Him.

This job was a position in a very prestigious firm and was yet another miracle that only God could have orchestrated. I did not make as much money as I was working in the clubs (and maybe when you are released you might have to take a job making less than you became accustomed to in your criminal career) but when you are in the Lord, and when you are faithful to tithe, He can make half as much go twice as far! We were experiencing fiery trials but along with those trials came wonderful miracles of God as well.

Persevering in the Faith

Now that the demonic strongholds in my life were losing their power God was teaching me how to put my trust in Him. We were still living in the projects and at times I would watch from my window as crowds would gather to see what a kid would do who was brandishing a gun. Of course, my boys would be right in the middle of it all. Every day I would cry out to God to get us out of there and at the same time I would praise Him for the fact that we had a place to live. In fact, I was praising God for everything. Praise is what redeems situations out of the hands of the devil! It would take a lot of money to pay a security deposit and the amount of rent that would be required for a decent place. That would take tremendous faith. But what is faith? I was beginning to learn that faith is actually what gives substance to the things that we hope for.

"Now faith is the substance of things hoped for, the evidence of things not seen" (Hebrews 11:1).

In other words, what God was teaching me is that faith is grasping the unrealities of hope and bringing things into the realm of reality. Well, I had faith to get off welfare, faith to get a good job, and I could have faith for moving out of the projects!

One day, as I was praying to God to move us out of the

projects, He told me to clean the apartment. I had lost interest and had not done a really good cleaning for awhile. Well, knowing that I had heard from God, I dug in. I cleaned everything from stem to stern until the place was ship shape! God calls us to be good stewards of the things we have.

"*His lord said unto him, well done, thou good and faithful servant: thou has been faithful over a few things, I will make thee ruler over many things: enter thou into the joy of thy lord*" (Matthew 25:21).

Bye Bye Projects

During this point in time my daughter married her sweetheart and they moved to a double home not far from the projects. Within a few weeks, the other half of the home became available. I had been saving my money and I had saved enough to move. Now you might be thinking, that's no big deal, so they moved, and from all outward appearances it wasn't a big deal. But I knew in my spirit the amount of power it took to liberate us from the prison and the hell of the projects. This was yet another miracle of monumental proportions. The house wasn't far from the projects but it was a home, not an apartment in the projects, and the neighborhood was better. Truly, we were on our way, working through the process by faith, to the promises of God.

Even though my daughter was only 16 and her new husband 18, they were both very mature. Kids grow up fast in the projects! Together we got the idea to save our income tax refund money, pool our resources by living on my son-in-law's paycheck and banking mine. Within three years we saw our way clear to purchasing a home. We had been delivered from exile and found ourselves back in the same suburb we came from. Two years later we moved again into a beautiful home in the country. We were learning how to use our faith to bring the substance of the things we needed into our lives. I would look around at the new Christians under whose discipleship God had placed us and think to myself that if God did it for them; He would do it for me. I knew I could have faith for anything God had for me. You might be asking yourself, what do houses and things have to do with victory in Jesus. Well, the reason I am relating these miracles to you is summed up in many Scriptures in the Bible but the Apostle John says it best.

> *"Beloved, I wish above all things that thou mayest prosper and be in health, even as thy soul prospereth" (3 John 2).*

Indeed, our souls were prospering. We were going to every Bible study we could find, devouring our Bibles, and praying. We were not only learning how to pray to God, but how to pray against the devil. Little by little we were all getting healthier and freer from the oppression that had us bound. We encountered many skirmishes because when you are as entrenched in the devil's camp as we were, he doesn't let go very easily, but let go he must.

Miracle Babies

> *"Children are an heritage of the Lord and the fruit of the womb is His reward.*
> *As arrows are in the hand of a mighty man; so are the children of the youth.*
> *Happy is the man that hath his quiver full of them" (Psalms 127:3-5a).*

After a couple years of marriage, my daughter and son-in-law had decided it was time to have a child. We felt strongly that the Lord was assuring us they would have a son and his name would be Israel but they were not having any success. After spending a week in the hospital the results of all the tests showed that Cherie was unable to conceive or carry a child. Our family doctor who told her the news was a Christian. He knew the Word and that they were believing by faith to have a child. "But, he said, "There was Sarah." Sarah is a woman in the Bible who believed and had a miracle baby. "Victor," she said, "That is what I am going to name my baby girl after I have my son Israel."

Shortly after being told that there was no way she could conceive or carry a child, at another miracle healing service my daughter felt her abdomen become very warm and she knew she was healed. Our miracle baby Israel was born the next year and the year after that came our miracle Sarah.

These miracles are only a few of the many my kids and I were experiencing on our way to victory from imprisonment and bondage. Now, we walk in the miraculous every day and just as we experience one victory and miracle after another, the same is promised to you. Hopefully in reading my story you can see yourself and some of the trials you have gone through. Hopefully you will begin to apply some of these principles of obedience in your own life that we did in ours so that you too can get free. Even though there may be fiery trials along the way, make the decision today that you will walk in the miraculous promises of God.

Surrendering and Applying God's Word to Your Life

I have shared my story with you because I want you to

see that no matter how much of a mess you find yourself in, no matter how hopeless it may seem there is hope for your future. Whether you are behind bars or behind the eight ball in life, God will make a way where there seems to be no way.

The way that God made for me required my total surrender to Him and applying His Word to my life daily. Surrender is a paradox, a contradiction in terms, because victory comes through surrender. Surrender doesn't weaken you; it strengthens you. Surrendered to God, you don't have to fear or surrender to anything else.

Now we will move on to the short teachings I have been telling you about. They are letters to you. Read them with hope and faith in God's promises. Read them and hold them close to your heart, apply them to your life right where you are so that when you are released, you will be able to withstand all the wiles of the devil and all the challenges you will face in the outside world.

CHAPTER 8

Salt and Light

Christians are Salt and Light

RECEIVING THE PROMISES of God and learning how to apply them are dependent upon some spiritual conditions. One of those conditions is that we must become aware of the fact that Christians are to be the salt and light in this dark world. In reading the Old and the New Testaments we can make some very important discoveries. One of them being that God created everything, including us. You have probably heard of the story of Adam and Eve which explains that we did not evolve from animals. What makes us different from the animals is that God breathed His Spirit into Adam. He didn't breathe His Spirit into animals. Animals have souls – they feel happiness, sadness, affection, and instincts, but they do not have free wills and are incapable of sin.

Through this man, Adam, sin entered into the world. Adam and Eve passed this sin nature on to their children. Our lives are extensions of Adam's life, so – as unfair as it seems – we too stand condemned before God just as did Adam and we have inherited death. But, we read in 1 Corinthians:

◀ REDEEMING HARD TIME AND HARD TIMES

"For since death came through a man, the resurrection of the dead comes also through a man" (1 Corinthians 15:21).

In verse 22 the Apostle Paul tells us who these two men are:

"For as in Adam all die, so in Christ all will be made alive" (1 Corinthians 5:22).

So through Jesus we have the good news of salvation. Just as Satan brought death through Adam, Jesus has redeemed us and brought, not only life through Himself, but He brought us eternal life. Although we had no choice in what Adam did to the human race, none the less we inherited it because we are his descendants and each one of us sins in our own right. Thank God that He loved the world so much that He gave us His son as a gift. But we must receive this gift if we are to benefit.

Christians are different from those who are in the world and of the world in that they have received the gift of salvation and have become born again. When a person is born again his or her entire worldview changes and he or she becomes the salt and light of the earth.

"Ye are the salt of the earth; but if the salt have lost his savour, wherewith shall it be salted? It is thenceforth good for nothing, but to be cast out, and to be trodden under foot of men.

Ye are the light of the world. A city that is set on an hill cannot be hid.

Neither do men light a candle and put it under a bushel, but on a candlestick; and it giveth light unto all that are in the house.

Let your light so shine before men, that they may see your good works, and glorify your Father which is in heaven" (Matthew 5:13-16).

But, what does it mean that believers are to be salt and light? Jesus used this concept several times when He was referring to the role of His followers. In Jesus' day, and in some places in the world even today, salt is used to preserve food when there is no refrigeration. Just like salt preserves food, Christians are to be preservatives in the world – preserving it from the evil that is so prevalent in these last days. You see, it is our presence in the world that is holding back the hand of God from allowing even more evil to run rampant in the world today.

Salt is also used then, and now, as a flavor enhancer. Like salt flavors food, Christians are to enhance the flavor of life in this corrupt world. When believers are living in obedience to God, they, much like salt, will be a positive influence in the world. It is the Christian who brings peace into a strife filled situation. It is the Christian who binds up wounds and brings help where it is needed. The good works of Christ's followers shine for all to see all over the world like a lighthouse in a storm. So we are to let our light shine and let our good works be light in the darkness.

Are you Fulfilling Your Role in Life?

Much of the problem today, however, is that many a believer is not fulfilling his or her role as salt and light. When you make choices that blur the distinction between us and the rest of the world it is a hindrance to our preserving power. When you make the decision to accept the ways of the world because it feels good, or because it is comfortable or more convenient than accepting the way that God would have you to go you compromise or settle for worldly things. You walk away from the Holy Spirit's leadings. Then, the "saltiness" in your life has lost its flavor and is no good to anyone.

The world is in great spiritual darkness. Why? Because the world is made up of sinners and sinners are ignorant of the true God. Many of them have a correct theory in some respects but they don't really know God. To know God is to have eternal life and while in their sins, mankind has no life beyond this one on earth. Sinners are in great darkness in respect to the spirituality of God's laws. If they understood they would know something of His character and of their own character as well. It is only possible to know about your own character if you know about God's.

Jesus is the source of light and Christians are to be the reflection of that light. Our function is to shine for Him just like the moon shines as it reflects the light of the sun. We should let our light so shine that as people see our good works we will glorify our Father. The way we live our lives for Christ speaks much louder than any words.

As you live your life for Christ as the salt and light in this dark world, you learn how to receive His promises. However, you can never hope to see the promises of God work in your life if you don't know what those promises are. You can never hope to know Him if you don't know who you are! You can never hope to get free from oppression or anything else and then hope to stay free if you don't know who you are in Christ.

Who You Are In Christ

Worldly speaking, you may have been someone who has

PART 1: WHAT IS CHRISTIANITY ANYWAY?

a checkered past. Maybe you have been in and out of jail, been a junkie, or an alcoholic, an abuser, homeless, and or living a meaningless existence. You may remember the TV program, "Life Styles of the Rich and Famous." Well some of you had life styles of the poor and aimless – But that was then, this is now! Things in your life have changed haven't they? But have they changed enough? Have they changed for the better? If you don't know who you are in Christ your life may not have changed as much as it could.

When you were in the world you didn't really have a clue as to who you were. Well, now you know that you *were* of your father the devil because that is who the Bible says you were. Now, however, you have a new Father, the Lord, but do you know just exactly what that means? Many Christians still don't know who they are in Christ. Do YOU know who you are in Christ? You see, the promises of God cannot work effectively in your life if you don't know what those promises are and you can't know who you are in Christ if you don't know what He has given you and what He has promised you. You can never hope to get free from oppression or anything else and then hope to stay free if you don't know who you are in Christ. Contrary to popular opinion the cartoon character, Popeye, was not the first one to say, "I y'am what I y'am. The Apostle Paul was. In 1 Corinthians he says:

"But by the grace of God, I am what I am, and His grace toward me was not in vain, but I labored more abundantly than they all, yet not me but the grace of God which was with me" (1 Corinthians 15:10).

Paul knew who he was in Christ. I challenge you to ask yourself, "Do I really know who I am? Do I really know Whose I am?"

Years ago a pastor told me, "What you need to do is to find out who you are in Christ because knowing who you are in Christ will put you on the path to receiving the promises of God. So I set out on a journey – a journey to learn just who I was in Christ. I had been a Christian for 10 years and thought I knew just exactly who I was for the first time in my life, but I wasn't sure I knew who I was in Him?

What We Say is What We Get

Our confessions rule us. When we use the word confession we are inclined to think of the negative side – the confession of our sins but the Bible has much to say about the positive side of this equation – the confession of our faith!

"Wherefore, holy brethren, partakers of the heavenly calling, consider the Apostle and High Priest of our profession (confession), Christ Jesus" (Hebrews 3:1).

Jesus, not the Saints, is the one who presents our confession before the throne of God. I decided I would rather He present my positive ones than my negative ones.

"If thou shalt confess with thy mouth the Lord Jesus, and shalt believe in thine heart that God hath raised Him from the dead, thou shalt be saved. For with the heart man believeth unto righteousness; and with the mouth confession is made unto salvation" (Romans 10:9-10).

"Thou art snared with the words of thy mouth; thou art taken with the words of thy mouth" (Proverbs 6:2).

PART 1: WHAT IS CHRISTIANITY ANYWAY?

"For verily I say unto you, that whosoever shall SAY to this mountain, be thou removed, and be thou cast into the sea, and shall not doubt in his heart, but shall believe that those things which he SAITH shall come to pass, he shall have whatsoever he SAITH.

Therefore I say unto you, what things soever ye desire, when ye pray; believe that ye receive them, and ye shall have them" (Mark 11:23, 24).

God's Word is very convincing when it comes to what we say. This principle was made crystal clear to me one morning several years ago. It was during the time when I was still struggling in what seemed to be hand-to-hand combat with devils and at a time when nothing seemed to be working. This particular morning I woke up and heard a voice in my spirit that seemed to come from right beside me in my bed. This is what I heard in my heart in a slow, deliberate, soft voice, a voice I knew to be God's: "You have come to a mountain in your life. You have tried going over the mountain, under the mountain, around the mountain, and through the mountain. But My Word says that you should SPEAK to the mountain." Wow, we make it so difficult, don't we?

You see, if you believe a thing in your heart, positive or negative, and you say it with your mouth often enough, you will really have it. It is always with the heart that man believes and with the mouth confession is made to any of the provisions and promises of God.

"Seeing then that we have a great High Priest that is passed into the heavens, Jesus, the Son of God, let us hold fast our profession" (Hebrews 4:14).

What is the confession we are to hold fast to – the confession we are to maintain? It is the confession of our faith in the Lord Jesus Christ!

Many Christians do not confess what God's Word says about them. They don't confess who the Bible says they are and that they have what the Bible says they have. In other words, they are not holding fast to their profession of God's promises and His provisions. A wrong confession is a confession of defeat, of failure, and of the supremacy of Satan. But many Christians fail in this area because of ignorance of what God says about who they are in Christ.

Do you find yourself talking often about what a bad time you are having? How the devil is keeping you from success? Keeping you sick? Holding you in bondage? As long as you continue to talk like that, according to what it says in Mark, you are in bondage because what you say is what you get!

"For verily I say unto you, that whosoever shall say unto this mountain, be thou removed, and be thou cast into the sea; and shall not doubt in his heart, but shall believe that those things which he saith shall come to pass; he shall have whatsoever he saith."

God is not a failure and defeat is not of God. Defeat and failure demand expression and testimony but so does faith. Yes, faith demands expression and testimony.

"And they overcame him by the blood of the Lamb, and by the word of their testimony" (Revelation 12:11).

Yes, it is by our words and the testimony of our faith in what Christ has done for us that we overcome. Faith finds its joy in our continual confession. Jesus was constantly confessing who He is, what He is, and what His mission was in coming here to earth.

We are children of God – sons and daughters of God, joint heirs with Jesus. We were born of God when we were born-again. He is our Father now, not the devil. We have to dare to take our places as sons and daughters of God and confess who we are in Christ. We did a lot of daring things back then before we were in Christ, didn't we? Well, let's get daring for God now!

When you know who you are in Christ you will know in what direction you are going, but, you might ask, how will I know? You will know the same way you know east from west, north from south, by using a compass. Well, the Bible is your spiritual compass. By reading the Bible you are learning how to read that spiritual compass to determine your spiritual direction. Today, we not only have compasses, we have Global Positioning Systems, GPS units. They not only tell us what direction we are going in but exactly where we are at all times. Now, did you ever think of the Bible as a GPS unit, God's Positioning System unit? The Bible, not unlike the GPS, tells us where we are at all times spiritually and also tells us where we are going.

The Bible is a mirror that reflects our image back to us so it is our job as Christians to use the Bible to find out what God's Word says about where we are and where we are going. The Bible also tells us WHO we are in Christ! But…you might retort, I have tried reading the Bible and I can't understand it, it doesn't make any sense to me. Have you ever noticed that people who are not Christians will tell you that?

The Bible is Not Just a Book

You've got mail! Don't complain that nobody writes to you because the Bible is God's love letter written right to you. The Bible is not just a book! It is the Holy Spirit going into your mind to clear up that stinkin' thinkin. The reason it may not make sense to you is because a love letter is written to one who is in a love relationship with the writer. If you are reading someone else's love letter, of course it doesn't make sense to you – but when you are in a love relationship with the writer it makes perfect sense. So, you see, the Epistles are love letters to you, you are God's love interest – the apple of His eye, the object of His affection.

When you read through the New Testament – primarily the Epistles, (the word epistle means letter) these are letters that have been written to YOU personally. As you read through these love letters (and that is what they are, love letters), you will find over 100 expressions such as "in Christ," "in Him," "in Whom," "through Whom," etc. Underline them or highlight them when you find them. Write them out, meditate on them and then, confess them. Begin to say: "This is who I am, this is what I am, and this is what I have in Christ."

Remember, it is by our words and our testimony of what Christ has done for us that we overcome. Faith finds its joy in our continual confession. Just as Jesus was constantly confessing who He was and is, what He was and is, and what His mission was in coming here, we must confess who we are in Him because He came here. Faith's confessions create realities. You see, everything the Bible says is ours is indeed ours legally because the Bible is a legal document, sealed by the Blood of Jesus. However, it is believing and confessing it which makes it a reality in your life.

We are New Creatures in Christ

"Therefore if any man be In Christ, he is a new creature, old things are passed away, behold all things are become new" (2 Corinthians 5:17).

Here's the confession in that: I am a new creature in Christ Jesus! I am a new type of being with the life of God, the nature of God and the ability of God inside me. A Christian is not renovated like you would renovate an old piece of furniture; rather he is a new creature – not just made over, he is a new creation, something that never before existed - not like an old mattress with a new cover, you are new through and through, inside and out! When we become born-again Christians we are actually a new species, there are no others like us.

Our spirit is born again the first time we confess Christ and mean it with all our heart. We receive salvation but it doesn't take us long to realize that our body is the same as it was and our soul, which is our mind and emotions, has a long way to go to become like Christ. No, we don't get a new physical body at salvation but we can look forward to having one someday because that is what the Bible promises will happen when we get to heaven. It is the man on the inside who is the new creation. The person you were is now dead and gone! The inward man (or woman) is the real you. You are a spirit, you have a soul, (your mind and emotions) and you simply need your body to carry the real you around while you are on the earth.

Our bodies are only earth suits. The only way we can get

here to earth is in one of these and the only way we can stay here is if our earth suit can sustain life. When our body, our earth suit gets too old or sick, we can't stay here, we must leave the earth.

As we hold fast to the fact that we have the very Life and Nature of God in us, the new man on the inside will be manifested on the outside through the flesh. We need to let this new man on the inside dominate our outward man. God is looking at the new man in Christ when He looks at us. We look much better in Christ than we do out of Him. We can't see each other in Christ; we look at each other from the natural standpoint but God looks at us IN HIM!

Flesh and natural human reasoning limit us to our own ability. We look to the circumstances – the problems circumstancing around us, the tests, and the storms and we say that we can't. The language of doubt, the flesh and the senses is I CAN'T, I haven't the ability, the opportunity, or the strength. I am limited. But the language of faith says I CAN.

"I can do all things through Christ, which strengtheneth me" (Philippians 4:13).

In our finite minds we say, "I am more than a conqueror if the circumstances are right." That is not what the Word says, however.

"Who shall separate us from the love of Christ? Shall tribulation, or distress, or persecution, or famine, or nakedness, or peril, or sword:

As it is written, for thy sake we are killed all the day long; we are accounted as sheep for the slaughter.

*Nay, **in all these things** we are more than conquerors through Him that loved us." (Romans 8:35-37).*

God Has Made Provision

Not only does God make provision for us, and supplies all our needs, he comforts us with His Word.

"But my God shall supply all your need according to His riches in glory by Christ Jesus" (Philippians 4:19).

Notice that it does not continue to say only if you have a paycheck. He says you are blessed.

"Blessed be the God and Father of our Lord Jesus Christ who hath blessed us with spiritual blessings in heavenly places IN CHRIST" (Ephesians 1:3).

Notice it does not say He is GOING to bless you but it says that He has already blessed you with spiritual blessings. That means that in Christ Jesus, from the time you are born again until you step out of your earth suit into eternity He has already made promises for provision for all your needs. EVERYTHING you need is yours NOW. Find God's promises and His provisions in His Word and make them a reality in your life by confessing and receiving them today.

Part 2
How Do We Come to Jesus?

CHAPTER 9

Coming to Jesus as Children

We are as Little Children Before Him

WHAT IS IT about the children coming to Jesus that touches us so deeply? Perhaps it is part of our sense of security when we feel like little children before Him. But now that we are adults, we need to see the following passage in Luke from an adult standpoint.

> *"And they brought unto Him also infants that He would touch them; but when His disciples saw it, they rebuked them.*
> *But Jesus called them unto Him and said, suffer little children to come unto Me and forbid them not, for of such is the Kingdom of God.*
> *Verily I say unto you, whosoever shall not receive the Kingdom of God as a little child shall in no wise enter therein"* (Luke 18:15-17).

What does Jesus mean when He teaches His disciples from this incident? In Luke little children coming to Jesus is definitely in the context of humility. We know that because, in the passage just before it in verse 14b, Jesus, speaking to the Pharisees and the Tax Collectors said:

> "...for everyone who exalteth himself shall be abased and he that humbleth himself shall be exalted" (Luke 18:14b).

Presumably, parents wanted Jesus to touch their babies in an act of blessing. The word translated "touch" in Greek is *hapto*, to make close contact, touch' as a means of conveying a blessing. In this passage the word may also convey the idea of "to hold." A number of times Jesus touches to bless and to heal In Matthew's account we read:

> "Then were there brought unto Him little children, that He should put His hands on them and pray and the disciples rebuked them.
> But Jesus said, suffer (an old word for allow) little children, and forbid them not to come unto Me for of such is the Kingdom of heaven.
> And He laid His hands on them and departed thence" (Matthew 19:13-15).

The background of this story may be the practice of bringing children to the elders or scribes for a prayer of blessing upon them. You can imagine the setting; parents bringing babies, and letting their toddlers run up to Jesus and Jesus would, with great joy, scoop them up and pray for them. When Jesus did this once, other parents saw it and came down toward Him. They wanted this for their children, too, as their children were often with them in the audience.

But the disciples would have none of it. After all, Jesus was about important business -- teaching and healing. They couldn't allow His work to be interrupted by mere children constantly running up. So they began to stop the little children, and tell the parents in no uncertain terms to stop them from coming to Jesus. We know the disciples rebuked the parents sternly by the Greek word used there. The word translated "rebuked" in Greek is *epitimao,* to express strong disapproval of someone.

It makes you wonder just exactly what the view of children was in Jesus' day. The question of how children are viewed in Jesus' culture is important if we are to interpret this passage correctly. The disciples rebuked the parents because women and children were viewed as unimportant in Palestine but Jesus was liberating them. The incident in Luke that involved children is a good example:

"Then there arose a reasoning among them, which of them should be greatest.
And Jesus, perceiving the thought of their heart, took a child and set him by Him.
And said unto them, whosoever shall receive this child in My name receiveth me and whosoever shall receive Me receiveth Him that sent Me for he that is least among you all, the same shall be great" (Luke 9:46-48).

The principle of the innocence of children was alien in the Old Testament. True, children were not held responsible for sin even up to nine years of age, but evil impulses are there from birth, maybe even from conception. Not until the Apostle Paul sets the record straight does the idea of the innocence of children even appear.

"Brethren, be not children in understanding: howbeit in

malice be ye children (have no malice), but in understanding be men" (1 Corinthians 14:20).

We are to be harmless as children but intelligent as grown men and women. While children were prized by parents -- male children especially -- in society they were largely ignored as unimportant. They were not considered worthy of much adult attention outside their families but Jesus changed all that.

"But Jesus called them unto Him and said, suffer (allow) little children to come unto Me and forbid them not, for of such is the Kingdom of God" (Luke 18:17).

Can you just imagine the scene: red faced disciples having arrogantly told off the parents and instructed them to control their children in the presence of such an important teacher as Jesus? Then Jesus rebukes the rebukers and calls the children back to Him. "Come here, children...." Jesus called to them -- while the frustrated disciples stood powerless to stop it. They are supposed to do crowd control and Jesus is keeping them from doing their job. What are they to do? The little children run past the disciples, over to Jesus and jump up into His lap and they snuggle up close to Him while He lays hands on them and prays for them. Soon all the children in the entire crowd have run up to Jesus and are crowding around Him, waiting for Him to touch them and pray for them as well. What a beautiful picture!

Why does Jesus let them come on this occasion when it doesn't seem like this is His normal practice? It seems Jesus wants to use this occasion to make a point; to teach His disciples, and us, an important lesson about the Kingdom of

God. He said the Kingdom of God belongs to such as these. He says that those who inherit or possess the Kingdom will be like these children.

Essential Characteristics of Christians

Just exactly what characteristic of children is Jesus pointing to as an essential characteristic of disciples? Well, there are several possibilities here: Now, remember that the twist in the parables is usually the point Jesus is trying to make. The twist comes because the world and its philosophies are so diametrically opposed to the mind of Christ. What characteristic of children is Jesus pointing to as an essential characteristic of His disciples and of us? Here are a few:

"Foolishness is bound up in the heart of a child" (Proverbs 22:15).

2) Openness, trust, and receptivity are some other characteristics of children that Jesus was pointing to. Children will come running to Jesus with complete openness and trust, and this is essential for adults coming to Jesus as well.

3) Humility. The disciples considered children to be unimportant. Yet to Jesus, the children's humble station in life was itself symbolic of the humility required to approach God. Infants can't do a thing to merit the Kingdom, yet they are a metaphor (representative and symbolic) of our receiving the Kingdom. Jesus was saying that anyone who will not receive the Kingdom of God like a little child will never enter it.

How are we to be as little children? Little children come to Jesus freely, openly, and humbly. They come to God with no posturing of worthiness like the Pharisees and the Sadducees.

Rather, they come because Jesus calls them to Him. You may not realize it yet, but you are a believer today because He called you. Children come in simple faith, like the tax collector, and like the fishermen in the Bible; no pretension, only openness and humility. These are the qualities of children that Jesus seems to be holding up as necessary for entrance into the Kingdom.

Okay, what are we to learn from all this? For one thing, we are to respect children and welcome them. Children are very spiritual little beings and can learn from an early age the truths of the Gospel. Jesus blessing the children shows His own respect for the spiritual life of children. For another thing, we learn that we, too, must come to Jesus without pretension and with humility and recognize that it is God's grace and mercy that allows us to approach the Lord. We can only enter the Kingdom when we come, like a little child, depending upon Jesus and not ourselves.

This is really good news if you have ever felt that Jesus would not welcome you because of something you did in your past or because you rejected Him for so many years. You see, coming to Jesus has nothing to do with your worthiness and everything to do with His willingness to forgive, cleanse, and transform you.

Run Into His Arms Like The Children

So, what this passage of Scripture is saying to us is this: If little children can run into the arms of Jesus why not you? Why not now? Maybe you have already come to Him and have received Him as your Lord and Savior and maybe He is calling you to deeper things, maybe a ministry, maybe simply to be a better son, a better daughter, a better husband, a better wife, or a better worker.

PART 2: HOW DO WE COME TO JESUS?

The world didn't think much of children, and maybe the world didn't think much of you either, but Jesus placed a great importance and value on children and He has placed a great importance on you. You see, it is not the way the world evaluates you that counts. Jesus placed such a great value on you that He died for you so you could be free from your sins and live eternally with Him.

There is no other you. When He made you He threw away the mold. He's got a plan that is tailor made just for you. If you trust Him like the little children did, and follow Him like the fishermen did, like the tax collector did, like so many others have I guarantee you He will take you places you never dreamed of.

Let's pray: Father, I have lots of history and baggage behind me that can be an obstacle and can hinder me from approaching you openly, humbly, and gladly but, when I see how Jesus welcomes the children, I can see that you welcome me too and I will to come humbly to you for salvation and deliverance, and I am ready for you to unfold your plan for my life. In Jesus name I pray, Amen.

CHAPTER **10**

The Prodigal Son

The Bible is a Mirror

WE USE MIRRORS to spot imperfections in us and also to notice improvements. James compares the Bible to a mirror.

> *"But be ye doers of the Word, and not hearers only, deceiving your own selves.*
> *For if any be a hearer of the Word, and not a doer, he is like unto a man beholding his natural face in a glass:*
> *For he beholdeth himself, and goeth his way, and straightway forgetteth what manner of man he was.*
> *But whoso looketh into the perfect law of liberty, and continueth therein, he being not a forgetful hearer, but a doer of the Word, this man shall be blessed in his deed"* (James 1:22-25).

James is teaching us that we are to live out the message of the Bible and not just listen to it. If you only listen to what it says and don't live out what it says it is like looking at your imperfections in a mirror and then walking away forgetting what you look like and what kind of person you really are.

REDEEMING HARD TIME AND HARD TIMES

Unlike your bathroom mirror, however, the Bible also shows us how to repair our flaws if we look close enough and don't walk away.

In this book we are going to take a look at some people who lived long ago but who we can still compare ourselves to today – kind of like looking into a mirror. This first story is called the parable of the prodigal son spoken of in Luke. This story is my story, your story, the story of every person who has strayed away from our Father God and was gathered to Him again when we came to ourselves and repented of our sin.

"And He said, a certain man had two sons:

And the younger of them said to his father, Father, give me the portion of goods that falleth to me. And he divided unto them his living.

And not many days after the younger son gathered all together, and took his journey into a far country, and there wasted his substance with riotous living.

And when he had spent all, there arose a mighty famine in that land; and he began to be in want.

And he went and joined himself to a citizen of that country; and he sent him into his fields to feed swine.

And he would fain have filled his belly with the husks that the swine did eat: and no man gave unto him.

And when he came to himself, he said, How many hired servants of my father's have bread enough and to spare, and I perish with hunger!

I will arise and go to my father, and will say unto him, Father, I have sinned against heaven, and before thee,

And am no more worthy to be called thy son: make me as one of thy hired servants.

PART 2: HOW DO WE COME TO JESUS?

And he arose, and came to his father. But when he was yet a great way off, his father saw him, and had compassion, and ran, and fell on his neck, and kissed him.

And the son said unto him, Father, I have sinned against heaven, and in thy sight, and am no more worthy to be called thy son.

But the father said to his servants, Bring forth the best robe, and put it on him; and put a ring on his hand, and shoes on his feet:

And bring hither the fatted calf, and kill it; and let us eat, and be merry:

For this my son was dead, and is alive again; he was lost, and is found. And they began to be merry.

Now his elder son was in the field: and as he came and drew nigh to the house, he heard music and dancing.

[26]And he called one of the servants, and asked what these things meant.

And he said unto him, Thy brother is come; and thy father hath killed the fatted calf, because he hath received him safe and sound.

And he was angry, and would not go in: therefore came his father out, and entreated him.

And he answering said to his father, Lo, these many years do I serve thee, neither transgressed I at any time thy commandment: and yet thou never gavest me a kid, that I might make merry with my friends:

But as soon as this thy son was come, which hath devoured thy living with harlots, thou hast killed for him the fatted calf.

And he said unto him, Son, thou art ever with me, and all that I have is thine.

It was meet that we should make merry, and be glad: for

this thy brother was dead, and is alive again; and was lost, and is found" (Luke 15:11-32).

We Are the Prodigal

As you can see, this is a story about a certain man who had two sons. God is the Father The younger son typifies the repentant sinner, the older son illustrates the person, who like the scribes and the Pharisees is unrepentant and ungrateful and full of resentment and rebellion.

In this Bible story the younger son is known as the prodigal son. Prodigal means one who is recklessly extravagant, who spends money wastefully. Sound familiar – I bet, in your day, you spent a few bucks recklessly on drugs and alcohol and God only knows what else. This son became tired of living in his father's house, rebelled against him and decided he wanted to leave. Can't you just hear it, "I'm sick of you telling me what to do all the time – I'm outta here; Give me my money." He didn't want to wait for his father to die, and so demanded his portion of his inheritance ahead of time. In this parable the father grants the son's request. It pictures God letting a sinner make his own bad decisions and go his own way. Having divided the inheritance between the two sons, the father watches as the younger son departs and sets out on a journey to a far country. His journey to a far county typifies a life of sin and selfishness and separation from God's love, fellowship, and authority. The sinner or backslider is like the young son who, pursuing the pleasures of sin, wastes the physical, intellectual, and spiritual gifts given to him by God.

The son proceeded to blow the whole inheritance. He squandered it on wild and crazy living. In today's world it would probably be spent on drugs, alcohol, partying, rounds at the bar every night, prostitutes, cars, boats, and gambling. In today's world it would be like someone who won millions in the lottery and a few years later is totally broke. You hear of stories like these quite often.

Then the parable says when he spent all his money there arose a famine in the land. He realized he was broke and found himself to be destitute. This scenario is pretty familiar isn't it? One day you may have found yourself destitute as well. He was desperate for a job but the only employment he could find was feeding pigs. He couldn't possibly sink any lower than that. You have to understand that a Jew working for a Gentile and caring for swine was unacceptable, very distasteful and disgraceful. You know, Jews don't want anything to do with pigs!

As he watched the pigs eating their bean pods, he grew to envy them. They had more to eat than he did and the Bible says that there was no one who wanted to help him. It is pretty bad when even unclean animals are better off than you. This is a picture of the lost sinner. Much like the lost sinner of today, he probably gave a lot of money to friends, bought them things, supplied them with drugs, alcohol, prostitutes – hey, isn't that what friends do? Isn't it interesting how that works? When you're out there spending money like crazy you have all kinds of friends but when you find yourself broke and destitute and you need them – they're nowhere to be found.

Coming to Yourself

The son begins to reflect on his condition and realizes that his father's servants have it far better than he. Eventually, the sinner discovers how desperate his situation has become as a result of his sin and realizes that to be outside of God's family is to be utterly alone. You see, before a sinner can come to God he or she must see that they are a slave to sin. Finally, the son decides to do something about it and devises a plan of action. He decides to confess his sin before his father. He says,

"I will arise and go to my father, and will say to him, "Father, I have sinned against heaven and before you" (Luke 15:18).

He determined to go to his father in repentance, acknowledging his sin, and seeking forgiveness. He felt that he was no longer worthy to be called his father's son, and planned to ask him for a job as a hired servant. Now the son was humble – even to the point of being willing to work for his father. You see, sinners have nothing to rely on except the Father's mercy.

So you see, this famine proved to be a blessing in disguise. It was what made him think. He hit rock bottom. Do you remember when you hit rock bottom? Have you hit rock bottom yet? Because, if you haven't, I sure hope you do soon. The Bible says, "But when he came to himself." That is what we need to do, come to ourselves because until we do, we are unable to come to the Father. When the son was still a long way off, his father saw him and had compassion on him. When Jesus was telling this parable He was picturing God the Father, not waiting for His shamed child to slink home, but running out to gather that child, shamed and ragged and muddied, into His welcoming arms.

Can you see your image in this mirror? Can you see that this is you? Long before the son reached his house, his father ran to him and fell on his neck and kissed him. This action

PART 2: HOW DO WE COME TO JESUS?

breaks all Middle Eastern protocol; no father would greet a rebellious son this way but as is often the case in the parables of Jesus, the twist in the story is what makes the point. So, the father drapes himself on his son's neck and is so pleased and thrilled to see his prodigal son return.

The son proceeds with his confession and tells his father that he is satisfied to be his father's slave. The father will have none of it and restores the son to full sonship. We know this because just then, the father interrupted him by ordering the servants to put the best robe on his son, put a ring on his hand and sandals on his feet. He also ordered a great feast to celebrate the return of his son who had been lost and was now found. Even the angels rejoice when one sinner comes to repentance.

"Likewise, I say unto you, there is joy in the presence of the angels of God over one sinner that repenteth" (Luke 15:10).

The young man was looking for a good time, but he didn't find it in the far country and neither did you. Just like him all you found was grief and sorrow. The son found what he was looking for only when he had the good sense to come back to his father's house and that is when we find what we are truly looking for too – that is when we find the only thing that will fit that God shaped vacuum we have inside us. The world makes everything so complicated and complex but coming to the Father is so simple and that is why we often miss it. Even a child can reach out to God.

The father ordered a feast to be prepared and a fatted calf to be on the menu. Fatted calves were saved for special occasions like the Day of Atonement, the day when the Jews asked forgiveness for their sins. The son came from destitution to complete forgiveness to total restoration – just like you did. That is what God's grace does for a penitent sinner.

It's All About Me

Now then, when the younger son came back the elder son had been laboring in the field, so he missed all the action but he became consumed with a jealous rage when a servant told him that his brother had come back. He then refused to participate in his father's joy. He whined and complained that his father had never rewarded *him* for his faithful service and obedience. He had never been given as much as a young goat. "But this son of yours," he says – wow, he didn't even refer to him as his brother, but said to his father "this son of yours. This son of yours who has devoured your livelihood with harlots, you killed the fatted calf for him, what about me. It's all about me, it's all about me. Talk about mirrors...

Now the brother who had been on the outside is now on the inside, while the brother who had been on the inside is now on the outside. You may notice a difference in how your old friends and even relatives treat you once you get right with God. They may be angry with you too, they may mock you and your new faith, but know that you belong to God now and no relationship is greater than that!

The father comes out to the angry brother and tries to calm him down. Son, he says, you don't understand, you are always with me, and all that I have is yours. It was right that we should make merry and be glad. For your brother was dead and now he is alive again, and was lost and now he is found. We must have joy when our brothers and sisters come home to the Father but you see, the older son is too self-consumed to be caught up in the joy. The story leaves us

PART 2: HOW DO WE COME TO JESUS?

hanging. The elder brother is left to contemplate the father's words. We don't know if he comes in to celebrate or not. It's an open ending. What will he do? What will you do?

The older son is a picture of the scribes and Pharisees who resented God's showing mercy to outrageous sinners. To their way of thinking, they had served God faithfully, had never transgressed His commandments when in actuality they were religious hypocrites and guilty sinners. They were blinded by their pride. A wise man once said, "There are none so blind as those who will not see." The scribes and the Pharisees were blind to how far away from God they really were. If they had only been willing to repent and to acknowledge their sins, the Father would have had a great celebration for them as well. There's that mirror again!

That's just what happened to you. You thought you were okay with God too or that your relationship with God didn't really matter. But, one day, you came to yourself, repented, acknowledged your sin, and were willing to be a servant. God interrupted you and said, but you are no longer a servant, you are my son. You were lost and now you are found and this calls for a joyful celebration! You know, it never says that the joy in the celebration of the son's return ever ended and the joy in the celebration of your homecoming will never end either. It will go on for all eternity.

CHAPTER 11

Zoë Life

What in the World is Zoë Life?

THE BIBLE TELLS us in 1 Timothy that we are to:

"Fight the good fight of faith; lay hold on eternal life, whereunto thou art called, and hast professed a good profession before many witnesses" (1 Timothy 6:12).

That means you have been called into a new life by God Himself. It is not He that you should be fighting against but the powers of darkness that would tempt you to doubt your salvation.

You've been *called,* you've been born again and you have a New Life! But what exactly does that mean? Many Christians, especially new Christians, don't really grasp what they have? We all know that being a Christian is a ticket to heaven when we die but do you know that this new life you have as a believer in the Lord Jesus Christ is *Zoë* in Greek, (pronounced zow ay) and it has the power to completely change your life NOW.

REDEEMING HARD TIME AND HARD TIMES

It means you don't have to go on living like you did before. Some new Christians find themselves in a continual battle with unbelief trying to grasp this new life but it is received as a free gift from God. You cannot earn it by being good. Let's look at what the Scriptures say about this new life in Christ. Where does it come from? How do we get it? What difference does it make anyway? Let's find out.

You see, *Zoë*, this Greek word for "life" is the root word of "zoo" and "zoology." *Zoë* is the state of existing and being animate. It is common to all mankind, whether saved or unsaved. For example, the Apostle Paul says to the idol worshipping Greeks at Athens:

"Neither is worshipped with men's hands, as though He needed anything, seeing He giveth to all life (Zoë) and breath, and all things"

"For in Him we live (zao – the verb form), and move, and have our being; as certain also of your own poets have said, for we are His offspring" (Acts 17:26 and 28).

Zoë can refer to an individual person's life while he is on the earth but in the Greek New Testament, *Zoë* has a special meaning. There it speaks of the life that is given to us by God. It comes through Jesus to those who believe the gospel. I'll give you another little grammar lesson here - In this usage, *Zoë* is often modified by the adjective *aionios* pronounced e on e ous. [English: eon] which means eternal, everlasting, endless. You see, Scripture shows us that the source of this *Zoë* life is God the Father and it goes on forever. In John 6:57 Jesus calls Him "the [zao] Father or the living Father. This indicates that *Zoë* life is the very life that God has in Himself.

So, you see, our God is alive and the main reason for the coming of Jesus was to give *Zoë* life to mankind and to cause mankind to enter into and partake of the very life of God. He tells us in John:

"...I am come that they might have life, and that they might have it more abundantly" (John 10:10)

Sin Separates us from God

Even before the ages of time began, God had promised to give *Zoë* life to man. What was man's greatest need? LIFE! Man was without life because of sin. The Bible makes it abundantly clear that we all were dead in our trespasses and sins. This death was alienation from God.

"That at that time ye were without Christ, being aliens from the commonwealth of Israel, and strangers from the covenant of promise having no hope and without God in the world:
But now in Christ Jesus ye who sometimes were far off are made nigh (near) by the blood of Christ" (Ephesians 2:12, 13).

Again in Ephesians we are told that we have been alienated from the life of God.

"Having the understanding darkened, being alienated from the life of God through the ignorance that is in them, because of the blindness of their heart" (Ephesians 4:18).

Just the same way sin alienates and separates us from our

heavenly Father, incarceration alienates you and separates you from your loved ones, from the outside world, and from everything that made you comfortable. When we are dead in sin it involves separation and alienation from God but it also involves opposition to God. Before you were saved, you were actually an enemy of God.

"For if, when we were enemies, we were reconciled to God by the death of His Son, much more, being reconciled, we shall be saved by His life" (Romans 5:10).

"And you, that were sometime alienated and enemies in your mind by wicked works, yet now hath He reconciled" (Colossians 1:21).

"For we ourselves also were sometimes foolish, disobedient, deceived, serving divers lusts and pleasures living in malice and envy, hateful and hating one another" (Titus 3:3).

"Having the understanding darkened, being alienated from the life of God through the ignorance that is in them, because of the blindness of their heart;
Who being past feeling have given themselves over unto lasciviousness, to work all uncleanness with greediness" (Ephesians 4:18, 19).

Clearly, the Bible is a mirror. When we look into it we see ourselves as we were, and we see ourselves as we become when we are in Christ. It is unmistakable - because of man's sin and rebellion, what we justly deserved was death, not life. You often hear people say, "I deserve it". If we got what we deserved, we'd get death. So, even though we <u>deserved</u>

death, God decided to give us *Zoë* life instead. What a wonderful and good God.

Not only did He give us life, He did it by causing death to fall on the only One who truly lived, Jesus. Through His death, God's judgment on sinners was satisfied. You see, it should have been us who died on that cross and went to hell. No other god arose from death and is now alive. No other god will answer prayer. No other god is good. Only the God of the Bible is God

A person receives *Zoë* life when he responds to the gospel with repentance and faith. The gospel is called

"...the Word of life" (Philippians 2:16a).

God actually offers to exchange His *Zoë* life for man's death. The gospel brings repentance and the gospel brings faith and the gospel brings eternal life:

"Verily, verily, I say unto you, he that heareth my Word, and believeth on Him that sent Me, hath everlasting life, and shall not come into condemnation but is passed from death unto life" (John 5:24).

"He that believeth on the Son hath everlasting life; and he that believeth not the Son shall not see life but the wrath of God abideth on him" (John 3:36).

Faith and Life are Connected

The Scriptures often connect faith and life. For instance:

"For God so loved the world, that He gave His only begotten

Son, that whosoever believeth in Him should not perish but have everlasting life" (John 3:16)

"But these are written, that ye might believe that Jesus is the Christ, the Son of God; and that believing ye might have life through His name" (John 20:31).

We pass from death to life at the moment we receive the gift of *Zoë* life.

"We know that we have passed from death unto life" (1John 3:14a).

"But God, who is rich in mercy, for His great love wherewith He loved us,
Even when we were dead in our sins, hath quickened us (made us alive) together with Christ, (by grace ye are saved;)
And hath raised us up together and made us sit together in heavenly places in Christ Jesus" (Ephesians 2:4-6).

"He that hath the Son hath life; he that hath not the Son of God hath not life" (I John 5:12).

The *Zoë* life we receive from Jesus is not something separate from Him. It IS Him! In fact, the *Zoë* life we receive is Jesus Himself, because Jesus IS life. Now do you think we understand it? No way! We will never understand it, but He if says it, we believe it and we've got it. That's all that counts. You know you have it because you know in your knower! That means you have a witness in your spirit that witnesses with the Holy Spirit of God. *Zoë* life is Jesus because He is life.

PART 2: HOW DO WE COME TO JESUS?

Jesus is the Way

Jesus is the only way, the only truth, and the only way to God.

"Jesus saith unto him, I am the way, the truth, and the life: no man cometh unto the Father, but by Me" (John 14:6).

"I am crucified with Christ: nevertheless I live; yet not I, but Christ liveth in me: and the life which I now live in the flesh I live by the faith of the Son of God, who loved me, and gave himself for me" (Galatians 2:20).

So what does all that mean? It means that being made alive in Christ transforms the course and outcome of our lives; not only in the here and now, but in eternity as well. Oh, we still have to live in a mortal body but we are not limited and bound by sin. It was so awesome when I first discovered that I didn't have to sin any more. I had the power in me to say no.

Our hearts have actually been changed. They go through a metamorphosis. We have passed out of one stage into another. I often will say of someone, oh, they'll be alright after the operation. What operation? The heart transplant! God gives us a new heart!

Many times you will see butterflies symbolizing Christianity. The reason for that is because, like butterflies, our lives actually go through a metamorphosis as God works in us. Our journey of transformation is similar to the one the ugly old worm goes through as he wraps himself in a cocoon and after a certain period of time, he emerges as a beautiful butterfly, completely unlike the ugly worm he was.

Don't you sometimes feel that way? Think about it. You were like an ugly worm bound up so tight that you could hardly move. It might have even felt like you were in a cocoon, and now you are free as a bird and as beautiful as a butterfly but that's not all! We not only have hope in this life, but in our everlasting life as well.

"If in this life only we have hope in Christ, we are of all men most miserable" (1 Corinthians 15:19).

Those who only have life in this world are miserable, but we have eternal life. We know what we have to look forward to. Because Jesus was resurrected, we will also be resurrected and when that happens our bodies will also be involved.

"Marvel not at this; for the hour is coming, in the which all that are in the graves shall hear His voice,
And shall come forth; they that have done good, unto the resurrection of life; and they that have done evil, unto the resurrection of damnation" (John 5:28-29).

Jesus knows His own and on the last day He is going to raise those who have eternal life and give us a glorified body.

"Who shall change our vile body, that it may be fashioned like unto His glorious body, according to the working whereby He is able even to subdue all things unto Himself" (Philippians 3:21).

So let's live NOW to the fullest because He has given us eternal life but let us also not take this Zoë life for granted, or be ignorant concerning it. Let us not trivialize it, forget it, neglect it, or turn it into clichés. Let us not doubt or disbelieve it, let it slip from our grasp, or surrender it to Satan, our enemy. Let us, instead, trust God's promises, believe His word, and live by faith.

CHAPTER **12**

Aliens

Who Are They?

THERE IS A lot of talk about aliens these days. Everyone is trying to figure out who they are and where they come from. Did you know that the Apostle Peter says that you and I are strangers and pilgrims (aliens) here on earth?

"Dearly beloved, I beseech you as strangers and pilgrims, abstain from fleshly lusts, which war against the soul" (1 Peter 2:11).

I hope that by now you have accepted Jesus and what He did for you on the cross and are indwelled by the Zoë life I spoke about in the last chapter. If so, then your new position as God's own possession sets you apart from the people of this world to become pilgrims in this world. You (and all Christians) now live in a place to which we do not belong, and our true citizenship is with Christ in heaven.

"For our conversation is in heaven; from whence also we look for the Savior, the Lord Jesus Christ" (Philippians 3:20).

The term conversation means citizenship or homeland. The Apostle Paul emphasizes that Christians are no longer citizens of this world; they have become strangers and pilgrims on the earth. What does all this have to do with me though, you might ask? Actually, we need to realize that what we have is so different from what we had before we got saved. You have something very special – and you ARE something very special now that you belong to God.

The Apostle Peter starts out by introducing an "alien" theme in the very first verse of his letter.

"Peter, an Apostle of Jesus Christ: to the strangers scattered throughout Ponus, Galatia, Capadocia, Asia, and Bithynia" (1 Peter 1:1).

The word stranger in that verse in the Greek is the word *para pi demos*. This is how he is describing the Christians in those cities. Put your city in that passage and realize that he is writing to you. The New Testament was translated from Greek into English. The Greek language has many more nuances and shades of meaning for words than English does and many of these meanings get lost in the translation. For example, have you ever heard of the Holy Spirit being called Paraclete? A ministry called parachurch? Or a physician's assistant being called a paramedic? Or a lawyer's assistant being called a paralegal? The suffix para means alongside of. The Holy Spirit comes alongside of us to help us, parachurch organizations come alongside churches to help with ministry, and paramedics come alongside doctors to help with situations that are medical in nature and paralegals come alongside lawyers to help them with legal matters. I know – another Greek grammar lesson. Hang in there and you will see the importance of your knowing this.

PART 2: HOW DO WE COME TO JESUS?

You see, *para pi demos* means an alien alongside, a resident foreigner, a pilgrim stranger or sojourner, a *by dweller*, someone dwelling alongside. Now, Peter is opening his letter by referring to Christians this way. Christians, being strangers and aliens means that we are different in a culture that is hostile to God. But, exactly how are we different? Remember what we learned about Zoë life? We're different because we have hope. Zoë life gives us hope for the future and that hope for the future changes the way we see ourselves in the here and now. Yes, we are aliens here and that should affect the way we live from day to day. Because heaven is our home, <u>hope</u> for the future is the key to our identity.

Just what makes us different? We are different because, unlike those in the world, we are indwelled by the Holy Spirit of God with Zoë life. We are aliens in a foreign, pagan land until Jesus comes and takes us to our real homeland, heaven. We are no longer a part of the world system. We are living alongside of those who are hostile to God. Most of all we are different because we have hope for the future – not only for the future here on earth, but for our future in heaven.

Trials are Temporary: Heaven is Forever

Hope is the great motivation in the Christian's life and hope is the reason that Christians endure suffering. Peter says it is only for a little while until God takes us to heaven.

> *"Wherein ye greatly rejoice, though now for a season, if need be, ye are in heaviness through manifold temptations.*
> *That the trial of your faith, being much more precious than of gold that perisheth, though it be tried with fire, might*

be found unto praise and honour and glory at the appearing of Jesus Christ" (1 Peter 1:6,7).

So, you see the trials you go through are trials of your faith and they are precious to God. When you come out the other end, you love Him even more because He was there with you in the middle of them and you know that He will see you through the next one. Peter goes on to say:

"Whom having not seen, ye love; in whom, though now ye see Him not, yet believing, ye rejoice with joy unspeakable and full of glory:
Receiving the end of your faith, even the salvation of your souls" (1 Peter 1:8, 9).

God is pleased because even though you have not actually seen God, you believe Him and rejoice. Peter assures us that at the end of all this persecution is the salvation of our souls. Peter is comforting the persecuted Christians in his day and he is comforting the persecuted Christians in our day as well. He is assuring us that no matter how badly we are treated, we must always keep in mind that it is only temporary and that we have hope for our future. He is showing us the way in which we must live *in view* of and in the middle of all these things we are now enduring. He is also calling us to live holy lives, no matter what comes our way.

"Wherefore gird up the loins of your mind, be sober, and hope to the end for the grace that is to be brought unto you at the revelation of Jesus Christ;
As obedient children, not fashioning yourselves according to the former lusts in your ignorance:

> But as He which hath called you is holy, so be ye holy in all manner of conversation;
> Because it is written, be ye holy; for I am holy" (1 Peter 1:13-16).

We are Citizens of Heaven

Peter is calling them, and us, to stand fast and live wisely and holy before God as we rub shoulders each day with non-Christians. He is telling us to abstain from fleshly lusts, live honestly before men, submit to authority, be free, but live godly, honor all men, love the brotherhood, and most importantly, fear God.

With our citizenship being in heaven, it is our first and primary citizenship rather than that of the United States or whatever country in which your earthly citizenship lies. Our first and primary constitution is the Holy Bible not the U.S. Constitution or the constitution of your country. Our first and primary King and Commander in Chief is The Lord Jesus Christ and not the US President or any other president, king, or prime minister. The cravings of our hearts are not to be for the treasures or the beggarly elements of the world but for the Kingdom of God. Indeed, we are aliens. The language and values and customs and expectations of this world feel foreign to us now. Something really radical has happened to us. God has caused us to be born again to a living hope—for another world, another, greater kind of existence. Paul, in the book of Colossians puts it this way:

> "For ye are dead, and your life is hid with Christ in God.
> When Christ, who is our life shall appear, then shall ye also appear with Him in glory.

Mortify (kill) therefore your members which are upon the earth; fornication, uncleanness inordinate affection, evil concupiscence, and covetousness, which is idolatry.

For which things' sake the wrath of God cometh on the children of disobedience" (Colossians 3:3–4).

Let me give you another King James grammar lesson here. This passage is talking about unholy desires, unhealthy affections; strong sexual desires and lust; the kind that makes you want to possess something simply so no one else can have it. It is also referring to having a form of distorted, misplaced or unlawfully strong desire focused on another's possessions or property, or even on another person. Idolatry is the worship of a physical object as a god and having an idolatrous attachment or devotion to it.

Jesus called us to fix our minds on radically different priorities than these. We're not to be anxious for what we will have to eat or what we will have to drink or with what clothes we will have to wear because our heavenly Father knows that we need all these things. Rather, we are to seek first His Kingdom and His righteousness; and all these things shall be added to us.

"But seek ye first the Kingdom of God, and His righteousness; and all these things shall be added unto you" (Matthew 6:33).

God has assured us that He will supply all our needs in the foreign land of the world if we keep our life focused on the Kingdom of God and His values and purposes. We are aliens and living like aliens is utterly necessary. It is a tragedy when an alien falls in love with the world. In the books of

Colossians and Philemon the Apostle Paul called Demas his fellow worker along with Luke and Mark but in his second letter to Timothy, wrote these terrible words,

"For Demas hath forsaken me, having loved this present world, and is departed unto Thessalonica" (2 Timothy 4:10).

Don't Throw Away Your Faith

It is a great tragedy when a professing believer throws away his or her faith and hope in the future world, renounces citizenship there, and lives for "this present world." It is a great tragedy when professing Christian aliens are absorbed into the world and give up walking by the Constitution of the Kingdom, give up loving the King, and give up pursuing the cravings of the Kingdom. When they do this they have no right to think that they will inherit the Kingdom. Living as aliens in the world is the only pathway to heaven. If you choose to be at home in the world and love the things of the world, you will die with the world. John said:

"And the world passeth away, and the lust thereof: but he that doeth the will of God abideth (lives) forever" (1 John 2:17).

Our eternal destiny hangs on our willingness to totally surrender to the will of God because the world is constantly calling us to its inebriating power. The Bible tells us that we must be sober and in our right mind because there is something about this present age and this present world that seeks to put us into mind altering, drunken states. When one is drunk he is out of touch with spiritual things. It's just about

REDEEMING HARD TIME AND HARD TIMES

impossible to connect a drunk with reality at all, let alone the reality of spiritual things. Being in love with the world puts you out of touch with the reality of the Spirit. You may have sobered up from all your addicting substances, but now you need to sober up from worldliness. You see, the only thing that will make you a person connected with reality is sobering up from the addictive, inebriating power of the world.

CHAPTER **13**

The Inebriating Power of the World

Worldliness Can Make You Drunk

THE BIBLE TELLS us, that as Christians, we must be in our right minds and be SOBER! Being sober and of a sound mind is a good way to avoid being seduced by and absorbed into this age, especially since we are hurtling toward the end of this age

What does "the world" mean anyway? The Bible warns us that we are not to be in love with the world but that might be easier said than done when you stop to think about how seducing and inebriating the things in this world are to us today. Have you noticed, even in your lifetime, how much more beautiful everything from cars to clothes have become? When you walk through the mall it seems every other thing that catches your eye is shiny, glitzy, and gorgeous. Material things seem to call out our name as we pass by the elaborate displays of merchandise. Satan knows his time is short and that is why he is pulling out the big guns. We want big cars, big houses, and lots of everything, even if in order to have it we go into debt or steal it. Being in love with the world and the things in it is what is referred to as worldliness. There is nothing wrong with desiring and having material things if we put God first and allow Him to provide them for us.

"But seek ye first the Kingdom of God, and His righteousness; and all these things shall be added unto you" (Matthew 6:33).

You see, worldliness is diametrically opposed to trust and affection for Jesus. It is the love of money, hunger for uninhibited sex, and a craving for power. That, however, is only the half of it. To have a worldly attitude is to be arrogant and prideful, it is living entirely in the natural world and placing no value whatsoever on the spiritual. Those who are worldly crave not only the material, but the pleasures of sin, thinking nothing of using and abusing others. They are self absorbed having no regard for the property of others or respect for their positions in life. Their sin nature draws them away from the truth of the gospel of Christ.

The Zeitgeist

Our warfare is not against mere worldly ways and things, but our warfare is against the spirit of the world. The Germans have a word for it: Zeitgeist. It refers to the spirit of the times or the spirit of the age, the general cultural, intellectual, ethical, spiritual and or political environment within a nation, a specific group or the direction and mood associated with an era.

The world in the New Testament is simply referring to unregenerate human nature wherever it is found, whether in a

PART 2: HOW DO WE COME TO JESUS?

bar, a crack house or in a church. It is whatever comes out of this fallen human nature whether it is morally indecent or morally respectable.

So many individuals in the world today are spiritually blind and unable to perceive the perils that threaten. Often this is the result of relying only on the intellect for decision making. People in this condition are not able to understand spiritual things. To be spiritually blind is a serious condition and the consequences can be eternally fatal. These individuals cannot see the dangers ahead.

We can all agree that even in view of the fact that some are blind to what is really going on in this world, there is something about the present age and the present world that tends to put you out of your mind and makes you high, drunk and inebriated with the material world that surrounds us. Why do you think the devil wants you whacked out on drugs and alcohol and drunk with the material world? So you are not living in reality, and so you are missing all the signs of the times.

One thing is clear about drunks – it is almost impossible to connect a drunk with reality and it is entirely impossible to communicate with them on anything but a very superficial level. That's the way it is when you get drunk on the world – it puts you out of touch with reality and of spiritual things. Only one thing will make you a person who is connected with reality and that is sobering up, not only from the addictive, inebriating power of drugs and alcohol, but also from the addictive, inebriating power of the world.

When you're drunk with worldliness, you're only thinking of the pleasures of the world; you don't have any taste for heaven and no desire whatsoever to pray. While you are incarcerated you probably don't get drunk, but there is a world and a culture of its own in prisons and jails and you can become inebriated with the subculture that exists there as well.

The wise inmate focuses on preparing for the outside world, on getting close to God, on getting as much Scripture in him or her as possible, redeeming this time. There will be a determination never to do anything that will result in incarceration again. Some will never touch another addictive substance again, while others may become tempted once released. Then there are those who will never again be tempted to become involved in getting high or drunk again but will indeed be tempted to resume drunkenness with the world.

Be Accountable to Someone

So, what can you do to prevent being inebriated with the world? What can be done for a person who is about to give up reality and the sound judgment of spiritual mindedness; who is about to give himself or herself over to the stupor of worldliness? Well, what do you do with an alcoholic? Or a drug addict? The answer is intervention.

If you or someone you know begins to be tempted to go back into old habits, seek out people who are in Christ who will stand in the gap for you, pray for you. We need to be surrounded by brothers and sisters who care if we are displaying destructive behavior. We need to be accountable to one another.

If you or a loved one is going to escape the inebriating effects of the world and be sober in a world that is drunk, oblivious and uncaring about the things of God then you need other people, people who will help you take the steps necessary to keep your mind sound and your heart sober so that you don't gradually slide into the subtle mental delusion that this world is what really matters, You don't want to lose your identity in Christ.

The pleasures of the world are mind-altering so you need people around you who are close enough to spot it if you start to show signs of getting drunk on worldliness. That is why you need to be in constant fellowship with other Christians. Fellowship with small groups of serious, committed Christians is what you need to combat the creeping, drunkening, mind-altering, deluding effects of this God-ignoring world. This kind of fellowship will keep you honest. This kind of close fellowship will deliver recurrent jolts of reality just when you need them. Christians were never meant to be lone rangers they are meant to be in close fellowship with one another So that the first stages of addiction to substances and to the world can be detected and lovingly confronted and remedied with the Word of God and the power of the Holy Spirit.

Spiritual Adultery

Worldliness is actually committing spiritual adultery. God has called His Church a peculiar people that needs to be separate from the world.

"Wherefore come out from among them, and be ye separate, saith the Lord, and touch not the unclean thing; and I will receive you" (2 Corinthians 6:17).

God desires a Church that is living in holiness in the fear of God.

"Having therefore these promises, dearly beloved, let us

cleanse ourselves from all filthiness of the flesh and spirit, perfecting holiness in the fear of God" (2 Corinthians 7:1).

Someone once said: "I looked for the Church and I found it in the world, and I looked for the world and I found it in the Church." If we try to win the world by being like the world the world will win us instead. God calls us a "peculiar people"

"But ye are a chosen generation, a royal priesthood, an holy nation, a peculiar people; that ye should show forth the praises of Him who hath called you out of darkness into His marvelous light" (1 Peter 2:9).

Peculiar people are powerful people! God has anointed us and set us apart. We must be a powerful people in these last days, God is calling apart a people who love the things of God more than the things of the world.

"Adulterers and adulteresses! Know ye not that the friendship of the world is enmity with God? Whosoever therefore will be a friend of the world is the enemy of God" (James 4:4).

Whoever therefore wants to be a friend of the world makes himself the enemy of God. You see, the true man or woman of God is heartsick, grieved at the worldliness of the Church - grieved at the way that even the Church has become inebriated with and tolerant of sin and worldliness. The true man or woman of God is disturbed that there is so little prayer in the church that pulls down strongholds of the devil. Jesus said:

"Ye are the salt of the earth: but if the salt have lost his savour, wherewith shall it be salted? It is thenceforth good for

nothing, but to be cast out, and to be trodden under foot of men" (Matthew 5:13).

What a fearful statement: "trodden under foot" Do we not see this today as the world is mocking and walking over all decency and everything we stand for? A.W. Pink, a noted evangelist and biblical scholar in the early part of the 20th Century, is quoted as saying,

> "The nature of Christ's salvation is woefully misrepresented by the present-day evangelist. He announces a Saviour from Hell rather than a Saviour from sin. And that is why so many are fatally deceived, for there are multitudes who wish to escape the Lake of fire who have no desire to be delivered from their carnality and worldliness."

You just can't be a Christian and a worldling at the same time. Allowing yourself to become inebriated with the world is vanity and death. The Bible is clear:

> "Love not the world, neither the things that are in the world. If any man love the world, the love of the Father is not in him.
> For all that is in the world, the lust of the flesh, and the lust of the eyes, and the pride of life, is not of the Father, but is of the world.
> And the world passeth away, and the lust thereof: but he that doeth the will of God abideth for ever" (1 John 2:15-17).

The Christian cannot take part in the world and its sinful ways! We have ceased to be citizens of earth's polluted cities; we are citizens of heaven. We have a home--but not in the palaces or haunts of the world. We have a house, not made with hands, that is eternal in the heavens! Our citizenship is in heaven. And we eagerly await a Savior from there, the Lord Jesus Christ! We cannot mix worldliness with divine truth. It is a deadly mixture! We need to be able to say with the Apostle Paul:

"But God forbid that I should glory, except in the cross of our Lord Jesus Christ, by whom the world is crucified unto me, and I unto the world" (Galatians 6:14).

All it takes is one drop of colored dye in water to cloud the entire glassful and all it takes is one drop of poison in a drink to kill you. The Christian who becomes seduced by the inebriating power of the world drinks these "poisons." Don't be a Christian who, seemingly without any anguish, indulges in the world's ways. The Bible tells us who we are as Christians, what we believe, why we believe it, and what we are to be drunk with and full of – the Holy Spirit of God.

CHAPTER 14

Stinkin' Thinkin'

What do you say To Yourself?

ONE OF THE most common skills learned in psycho-therapy today focuses on our thinking. Unbeknownst to many of us, we often engage in internal conversations with ourselves throughout the day. Much of this thinking is what got us into trouble in the first place because much of it is lies. Unless we're trained to examine these inner conversations, however, many of us don't even realize we're having them and what is worse, we don't realize that much of it consists of misinformation that causes internal turmoil.

What we do not recognize is that there is a connection between our feelings, and thoughts, and the ongoing talking we engage in with ourselves. We actually feel the way we think, therefore if your thinking is off, the way you feel is too. When you start to listen to what you are saying to yourself you can begin to control your emotions.

For instance, imagine looking in the mirror at yourself. What's the first thing you think? That thought is a part of your internal conversation. Having these kinds of conversations with yourself is perfectly normal and in fact, everybody does it. Where we mess up in our lives is when we let these conversations take on a life of their own. If we answer ourselves with something like, "I'm fat and ugly and nobody loves me," that's an example of what I call "stinkin' thinkin'." Our thoughts have taken on an unhealthy attitude, one that is working against us instead of for us. Psychologists would call these thoughts "irrational," because they have little or no basis in reality. For instance, the reality is that most everyone is loved by someone (even if they're no longer with us), and a lot of our beauty springs from inside us — our personality and our character.

It is exactly these kinds of thoughts that you can learn to identify as you go through your day. It might even be helpful to keep a little journal of your thoughts, writing down the day and time you had them, the thoughts themselves, and the types of irrational thoughts — or stinkin' thinkin' that you have engaged in.

Stop Lying to Yourself!

As you learn to better identify these destructive thoughts you can then learn how to start answering them back with rational arguments. This is the way that you can work to turn your internal conversations back to being positive in your life, instead of negative. This is how you can change the stinkin' thinkin' and change your emotions and the very image you have of yourself.

There are several types of stinkin' thinkin.' There is all-or-nothing thinking where you see everything as either black-or-white and if a situation isn't perfect, you see it as a total failure. For example, when a person is on a diet and they eat a spoonful of ice cream, he or she tells themselves, "I've blown my diet completely; I will *never* lose weight." This thought can sometimes upset the person so much that they do something like gobbling down an entire quart of ice cream in one sitting.

Then there is overgeneralization where you see a single negative event, such as when someone rejects you or maybe a demotion at your job, as a never-ending pattern of defeat. We do this by using words such as "always" or "never" when thinking about it. Maybe you discover your girlfriend walking down the street with another guy; it is obvious that they are more than just friends. You say to yourself, "Just my luck! I can *never* keep a girlfriend!"

In negative reality thinking you pick out a single negative detail and dwell on it so that your vision of reality becomes off color or darkened, like the drop of ink that discolors a glass of water. For example: You receive many positive comments about how you look that day. One person says something mildly critical and instead of focusing on all the positive things people said you obsess about the one person's negative remark and ignore the positive ones.

If you reject positive experiences by insisting that they don't count you could do a good job at something but you tell yourself that it wasn't good enough or that anyone could have done it just as good. By doing this you take the joy out of life and you feel inadequate, and rejected.

Jumping to Conclusions

Then, there are those who jump to conclusions too quickly and interpret things negatively when there are no facts to support the conclusion. This is a common one. For instance, without even checking it out, you imagine that someone is reacting negatively to you. Or maybe you decide ahead of time that things will turn out badly. Before a test you may tell yourself, "I'm really going to blow it this time. What if I fail?" If you're depressed you might tell yourself, "I'll *never* get better."

Maybe you engage in magnification thinking where you exaggerate the importance of your problems and your shortcomings, or you minimize the importance of your good qualities. Or perhaps you use your emotions to reason where you assume that your negative emotions reflect the way things really are: "I feel terrified about going on airplanes. It must be very dangerous to fly." Or, "I feel guilty. I must be a rotten person." Or, "I feel angry. This proves that I'm being treated unfairly." Or, "I feel so inferior. This means I'm a second rate person." Or, "I feel hopeless. I must really be hopeless." Feelings are not always a good gauge of what is real, especially negative feelings.

Shoulda, Woulda, Coulda

How about "Shoulda"," woulda", "coulda" thinking. We are all guilty of this kind of thinking from time to time. This is where you tell yourself that things should be the way you hoped or expected them to be, if only you would have done something differently that you could have done. For example, after playing a great game of golf a gifted golfer tells himself, "I shouldn't have made so many mistakes." Musts, oughts, I have tos and the if onlys are other negative things we tell ourselves. These kinds of thoughts that are directed against ourselves lead to guilt and frustration and those directed against other people or the world in general, lead to anger and frustration.

Many people try to motivate themselves with shoulds and shouldn'ts, as if they were delinquent kids who had to be punished before they could be expected to do anything. "I shouldn't eat that doughnut." This usually doesn't work because all these shoulds and musts make you feel rebellious and you get the urge to do just the opposite. One time God spoke and revealed to me that I was playing God when I engaged in this kind of thinking. After all, He is the one who is in charge, not me or you.

Don't Give Yourself a Negative Label

Labeling is an extreme form of all-or-nothing thinking. Instead of saying "I made a mistake," you give yourself a negative label such as, I'm a loser. You might also label yourself as a fool, a failure or a jerk. Labeling is quite irrational because you are not the same as what you do. What you do is not who you are! By reading the Bible you find out who you are – if you are born again, you are a child of the Living God!

Labels are just useless abstractions that lead to anger, anxiety, frustration and low self-esteem. You may also label others. When someone does something that rubs you the wrong way, you may tell yourself: He's a jerk. Then you feel that the problem is with that person's character instead of with their thinking or behavior. You see them as totally bad. This makes you feel hostile and hopeless about improving things and leaves very little room for constructive communication.

Are you Really Responsible?

Before you take personal responsibility for something that went wrong, stop and analyze the situation. Ask yourself, "Am I really responsible for this situation?" You may be holding yourself personally responsible for an event that isn't entirely under your control. Say someone in your company dropped an expensive piece of equipment and it breaks. You placed the item on a table earlier and so you decide it must be your fault, because if you would have handed it to the person he may not have dropped it. Actually, you could not be responsible because the person picked the item up long after you placed it on a table but you condemn yourself anyway.

Some of the students I work with feel that if they get less than an A or a 4.00 GPA, (grade point average) then they are complete failures. This kind of thinking leads to guilt, shame and feelings of inadequacy. For this reason I begin each semester by telling the new students that it would be sinful for some if they did not get all A's but for others, who have many other family, ministry, and employment responsibilities, it would be sinful if they did get all A's because it would show that they were not spending enough time with other, more important obligations. You must remember that it's not all about you!

Some people do the opposite. They blame other people or their circumstances for their problems, and they overlook ways they might be contributing to the problem: "The reason my marriage is so lousy is because my spouse is totally unreasonable." Blame usually doesn't work very well because other people will resent being blamed and they will just toss the blame right back in your lap.

We create a lot of our own circumstances, whether good or bad, consciously, or unconsciously. Because not much happens by chance, most things, good or bad, come into our lives as a result of the thoughts we engage in, or by what God ordains to get our attention. It's easy to blame someone, or something outside of ourselves, and make excuses as to why we may be experiencing certain unpleasant situations. We need to be mature enough, however, to take full responsibility for our own lives and quit playing the part of the victim. It's liberating when you can say, "I got myself into this, and with God's help, I can get myself out!" There is no power in acting like a victim.

Right Thinking versus Wrong Thinking

Think the right way instead of the wrong way. You will see your conditions begin to improve. It's not the circumstances that get us as much as the way we react to them. Right thinking is thinking the way the Bible tells us to think. It is thinking about yourself the way the Bible says you should think about yourself. The Bible is the truth. That is why you must read it. It holds the truth about everything in life.

Wrong thinking has to do with our emotions. Since emotions are all over the place, they can't be trusted. Making decisions during an emotional high or low can and does get us into trouble and can be a recipe for disaster! Never make an important decision based on emotion. Rather, think it through and maybe the next day the same situation will look entirely different to you. The old saying, "sleep on it" isn't such a bad idea!

Thought is the Seed of Destiny

As long as we go on thinking wrong thoughts about ourselves and our lives, the same sort of difficulties will continue to harass us. Every seed must inevitably bring forth after its own kind, and thought is the seed of destiny. Let me repeat that...thought is the seed of destiny. When we think right thoughts by doing and saying what God's Word says about our situations, sooner or later, ill health, poverty, loneliness, and disharmony must disappear.

"For as he thinketh in his heart, so is he" (Proverbs 23:7).

Before we know God, and our eyes are opened to the reality that there really is a devil, we think our thoughts all originate within us. They do not. Our thoughts come from three different sources, ourselves, God, and the devil. God wants to influence us to have good thoughts.

"Finally, brethren, whatsoever things are true, whatsoever things are honest, whatsoever things are just, whatsoever things are pure, whatsoever things are lovely, whatsoever things are of good report; if there be any virtue, and if there be any praise, think on these things" (Philippians 4:8).

As long as there is a devil who also wants to influence our thoughts, we must constantly be aware that he is always trying to get you to agree with him so he can control you.

Pay attention to your thoughts for just one day, even writing them down. Then make a conscious effort to bind and cast down the negative ones. The way we think deserves our full attention. We can manage our thoughts and use them to create a better quality of life, or we can create a negative state of mind. We need to master the power of our thoughts. It is Christian warfare to bring all our thoughts into alignment with the will of God. Failure to do so will lead to immorality and spiritual death. (There's that stinkin' thinkin' again).

We need to agree with God and speak God's Word, in

faith, concerning every aspect of our lives. God knows our every thought and nothing is hidden from Him anyway. Our minds are a battleground. Some thoughts originate with us, some come from God, and some come from the devil. Therefore, it is vitally important to fill our mind with God's Word.

"For though we walk in the flesh, we do not war after the flesh:
For the weapons of our warfare are not carnal, but mighty through God to the pulling down of strongholds;
Casting down imaginations, and every high thing that exalteth itself against the knowledge of God, and bringing into captivity every thought to the obedience of Christ" (2 Corinthians 10:3-5).

CHAPTER **15**

What is Forgiveness?

It's Not a Feeling

WHEN I ASK Christians what forgiveness really is, most of them say, "I don't know." I have found that most Christians really don't know that rather than being merely a feeling, forgiveness is an act of our will. It is a choice to let go of anger, revenge, bitterness and resentment. It could be a feeling, and sometimes does become a feeling, but we are to forgive with an act of our will first, then perhaps the feeling will come.

Forgiveness is one of the most compassionate things that we can do. It is greatly misunderstood and because of this it is rarely given in the truest sense of the word. We often think of forgiveness as an act of kindness that we choose to give to people who are deserving of it and withhold it from those who are not. This gives us a sense of power when in actuality the power comes when we grant forgiveness to everyone who has done embarrassing, annoying, hurtful or vengeful actions against us, regardless of whether they "deserve" it or not. You see, forgiveness has very little to do with the other person, but it has everything to do with you! Forgiveness is a decision. It is a decision to release someone from your judgment and forgiveness is also the way to release you from bondage.

Forgiving Yourself

There is also a tendency in all of us to have unforgiveness toward ourselves holding ourselves more accountable than we do others. Forgiving yourself, however, is essential before you can forgive others. Perhaps you have been one who can justify forgiving others, even for a heinous offense, yet you find no justification for forgiving yourself for an equal or lesser offense. Perhaps you believe that forgiving yourself is not even a consideration because you think you must hold yourself in a state of life-long penance that you must pay. When the question was asked of Jesus,

"Master, which is the great commandment in the law? Jesus said unto him, thou shalt love the Lord thy God with all thy heart and with all thy soul, and with all thy mind.
This is the first and great commandment.
And the second is like unto it, thou shalt love thy neighbor as thyself" (Matthew 22:36-39).

Jesus was not commanding us to love ourselves here, He was merely pointing out that it is obvious we already do. So, yes, we should love ourselves. To not love ourselves would be wrong. Forgiving yourself is not specifically addressed in the Bible, but there are principles regarding forgiveness that should be applied here. When God forgives us, it states that He remembers our sins no more.

PART 2: HOW DO WE COME TO JESUS?

"...for I will forgive their iniquity, and I will remember their sin no more" (Jeremiah 31:34b).

This does not mean that our all-knowing Father God forgets, but rather, because He forgives us, He chooses not to bring our sin up again.

"Then Peter opened his mouth and said, of a truth I perceive that God is no respecter of persons" (Acts 10:34).

God shows no partiality, no bias, and no prejudice. He does not choose to forgive one person and not another so neither should we. He forgives everyone who believes in Jesus Christ. It is just as important to forgive ourselves as it is to forgive others.

Well, that is easier said than done, you might say, how can I begin the process of loving and forgiving myself and then begin loving and forgiving others? You can start by acknowledging your inner pain. Cry out to God to help you. He will show you the way. Tell Him how and why you hurt. He already knows, so it isn't any secret to Him but it will do you a world of good to tell Him and get it off your chest. Ask God to help you to replace your anger and unforgiveness with compassion for those who have hurt you, and compassion for yourself as well. Ask God for forgiveness for your role in any situation that has harmed you. We tend to forget that God is alive, and He will hear us and help us when we call on Him.

We also need to know what forgiveness is not. It is not forgetting or pretending it didn't happen. Whatever happened, happened. There is no undoing it. As long as we learned a good lesson from a situation it did not happen in vain. However, we need to have learned the lesson without holding on to the pain.

Forgiveness is not excusing the offense. We excuse someone when they are not to blame, but we forgive because a wrong was committed against us. Forgiveness is also not reconciliation. We have to make another separate decision about whether or not to reconcile. In many instances it is better to remain at a distance, especially if the relationship was a toxic one. It is not easy to forgive and let go of serious offences but it is a lot more stressful to hold on to those grudges.

Writing Letters Can Heal

If you are having trouble forgiving someone, write them a letter telling them that what they did to you has affected you and how you feel about it. Explain that you are releasing him, her or them from your judgment and letting go of unforgiveness. You don't need to mail it - in fact it is probably better that you don't - just write it and see how it helps you to just "get it all out." You will be amazed at how much healing will come as a result of letting go. To continue to rehearse in our thoughts the events of transgressions, opposes the Word of God. Remember, we are to think on good things.

Finally, brethren, whatsoever things are true, whatsoever things are honest, whatsoever things are just, whatsoever things are pure, whatsoever things are lovely, whatsoever things are of good report: if there be any virtue, and if there be any praise, think on these things" (Philippians 4:8).

Forgiveness is a Choice

The energy it takes to harbor anger, hatred, and resentment towards ourselves or others is exhaustive. Every bit of energy we give to negative activities such as dwelling on regrets and the sins and past actions of ourselves or of others, will rob us of the energy we need to grow in Christ.

Life is full of choices and forgiveness is one of them. Every choice we make takes us in a direction. We will either go in a positive, life-giving direction or allow the devil to rob us of the life that God wants us to live. Forgiving does not let us or others off the hook, however, and it does not justify what we have done, or what others may have done to us. Forgiveness is not a sign of weakness, but a sign of strength of character. Forgiveness is a choice that takes courage and it makes us overcomers rather than victims. When we reject the forgiveness that is given to us by God and when we refuse to forgive ourselves, what we are doing is setting ourselves above others and that amounts to pride!

"Pride goeth before destruction, and a haughty spirit before a fall" (Proverbs 16:18).

Unforgiveness of oneself will bring self-destruction, a haughty spirit, and a fall. Christian forgiveness will bring peace. Forgiving yourself is also important for those around you. It is a well-known fact that people who are hurting will in turn hurt others. The longer you avoid forgiving, the longer you allow yourself the stinkin' thinkin' of harboring the feeling that you deserve to suffer for what you did, or that the other person deserves to suffer for what he or she did. Holding onto that grudge could cause you to become explosive, and the quicker you will be to turn around and hurt others.

The reality is that you cannot change what has happened. You cannot restore lives to where they were before the event. However, you can make a difference in your life and the lives of others. You can give back some of what you have taken by investing your time and energy in compassion and forgiveness.

Forgive Yourself and Let the Healing Begin!

Forgive yourself and let the healing begin! Forgiving yourself will change the direction of your life. You have the power to be miserable for the rest of your life and you also have the power to give yourself permission to heal. God understands that pain causes our hearts and minds to close but there are other ways to adjust to what has happened to you. More depends on how you react to pain than the actual pain itself. You can remove the things that are blocking your path to living your life according to God's plan. If you don't know where to begin, here is a prayer that will get you started:

Dear Lord, I come before you humbly and give up my pride of unforgiveness. Now that I understand more fully the meaning and power of forgiveness I can see that there is nothing to gain by holding myself or others in its grip. I can also see now that there is everything to gain by releasing myself and others from unforgiveness. I want to begin the process of healing these wounds and I want to move forward and make a positive change in my life for my future. I confess all the pride and selfishness of holding myself and others in the bondage of unforgiveness. Because Jesus died for the forgiveness of my sins, I choose to forgive myself and to no longer punish myself and be angry with myself. I forgive myself for letting this hurt control me and for hurting others out of my hurt. I repent of this behavior and my attitude. I ask for Your forgiveness and healing. Lord, help me to NEVER again retain unforgiveness of myself or others. Thank you for loving and forgiving me. I pray this in Jesus' Name, Amen.

Part 3
Spiritual Warfare

CHAPTER 16

There's a War Going On!

The War is Unseen

THE SPIRITUAL WAR we are engaged in may be unseen but it is very real none the less! The big problem, however, is that there are so many Christians who feel helpless. We need to realize that God has not left us without weapons to fight in this battle. He has even given us orders to come against our enemy head on.

> *"For we wrestle not against flesh and blood, but against principalities, against powers, against the rulers of the darkness of this world, against spiritual wickedness in high places"* (Ephesians 6:12).

But what does all that mean? You can see, by reading this Scripture, that the Christian faces a spiritual conflict with Satan and many of his evil spirits. These powers of darkness are a vast multitude and are organized into a highly effective kingdom, a realm of evil with rank and order. These evil beings are continually attacking believers and are the spiritual rulers of the world and will be until Jesus returns.

REDEEMING HARD TIME AND HARD TIMES

Maybe you didn't know that the real war is not here on earth, but it is being waged in the heavenlies, and felt here on earth. In fact, we can feel it all around us. I will go a step further and say that we can actually feel it in us! Well, there really is a spiritual war going on. There has always been a war being waged against Christ but we are living in a time when the enemy is becoming bolder every day! Few Christians actually realize that there are very real, evil spiritual forces at work to rob, kill, and to destroy everything that Christ and His followers stand for.

"The thief (Satan) cometh not, but for to steal, and to kill, and to destroy: I (Jesus) am come that they (Christians) might have life, and that they might have it more abundantly (John 10:10).

"Behold, I give unto you power to tread on serpents and scorpions (devils), and over all the power of the enemy: and nothing shall by any means hurt you" (Luke 10:19).

Many people get involved in various religions because they are promised power. If you want real power, you must turn to Christ. He is the one with the real power and He gives it to us to fight in this unseen war. What many Christians don't understand is that the battlefield is them. They are getting beaten up by the enemy; physically, with poor health, financially with business problems, debt, joblessness, etc., in relationships within families, with coworkers, in their personal lives with what seem like hopeless addictions, bad habits like habitual crime and incarceration, and many other areas as well. These situations can be extremely perplexing to many Christians who have, perhaps, prayed and prayed about these circumstances but the problems remain. The word, circumstance means things standing in a circle around you, hemming you in. Don't you feel that way sometimes?

There may be a war going on, a war for our very souls, but God has not left us here without weapons to fight in this battle. These weapons, however, are not guns, knives, or fists. They are not carnal – of the flesh. These spirit being enemies have to be fought with spiritual weapons.

"For though we walk in the flesh we do not war after the flesh;

For the weapons of our warfare are not carnal, but mighty through God to the pulling down of strongholds. Casting down imaginations, and every high thing that exalteth itself against the knowledge of God and bringing into captivity every thought to the obedience of Christ" (2 Corinthians 10:3- 5).

Your Real Enemy is Satan

You see, to get the victory over these spiritual enemies, we must get rid of sin, pull down the strongholds in our minds, and cast down all the thoughts that are not godly and pleasing to God.

Many believers have been lulled into a spiritual laziness and do not exert the discipline or energy that is required to enjoy great spiritual victories. Yet, the Bible makes it plain that such discipline is absolutely necessary.

"But the fruit of the Spirit is love, joy, peace, longsuffering, gentleness, goodness, faith:

Meekness, self-control: against such there is no law" (Galatians 5:22-23).

"And take heed to yourselves, lest at any time your hearts

be overcharged with surfeiting (overindulgence) and drunkenness, and cares of this life, and so that day come upon you unawares.

For as a snare shall it come on all them that dwell on the face of the whole earth:

Watch ye therefore, and pray always , that ye may be accounted worthy to escape all these things that shall come to pass, and to stand before the Son of Man" (Luke 21:34-36).

"Therefore let us not sleep, as do others; but let us watch and be sober" (1 Thessalonians 5:6).

"Wherefore gird up the loins of (strengthen) your mind, be sober, and hope to the end for the grace that is to be brought unto you at the revelation of Jesus Christ;

As obedient children, not fashioning yourselves according to the former lusts in your ignorance:

But as He which hath called you is holy, so be ye holy in all manner of conversation. Because it is written, be ye holy; for I am holy" (1 Peter 1:13-16).

You see, if you call yourself a Christian, you are to live as holy a life as you possibly can and the only way to do that is by living a godly life as free from sin as possible. This is spiritual warfare! The first step in winning in this battle is getting saved. Salvation is like a helmet that protects your mind and it is one of the weapons of our warfare. All you need to do to put on this helmet of salvation is to say with your mouth that Jesus Christ is the Son of God and believe in your heart that God raised Him from the dead when He died for our sins and you will be saved.

"If thou shalt confess with thy mouth the Lord Jesus, and shalt believe in thine heart that God hath raised Him from the dead, thou shalt be saved. For with the heart man believeth unto righteousness; and with the mouth confession is made unto salvation (Romans 10:9, 10).

Make it a habit to read at least one chapter of the Bible everyday as this is also another of the weapons of our warfare. Apply what it says to your life and determine to stop doing things your way but His way instead because His ways are higher than ours.

Let the wicked forsake his way, and the unrighteous man his thoughts and let him return unto the Lord, and He will have mercy on him; and to our God, for He will abundantly pardon.
For my thoughts are not your thoughts, neither are your ways my ways, saith the Lord.
"For as the heavens are higher than the earth, so are my ways higher than your ways, and my thoughts than your thoughts" (Isaiah 55:7-9).

Always remember this: when the Bible refers to "he" and when it applies such as it does in this last verse, God is referring to mankind, men and women. When you begin to read the Word of God daily, you will be amazed at how much of the Bible will speak to you on a personal level. Apply the teachings to your life and to your mind. Reading the Word of God cleanses and renews your mind. It will teach you what is in God's mind. It will show you how God wants you to think. Learning how to think in the right way is warring against the enemy of your soul and it is spiritual warfare of the highest order.

The Immoral will not see God's Kingdom

"For God hath not called us unto uncleanness, but unto holiness" (Thessalonians 4:7).

"Abstain from all appearance of evil" (1 Thessalonians 5:22).

"Now the body is not for fornication, but for the Lord; and the Lord for the body (1 Corinthians 6:13b).

"Know ye not that your bodies are the members of Christ? Shall I then take the members of Christ, and make them the members of an harlot? God forbid.
What? Know ye not that he which is joined to an harlot is one body? For two, saith He, shall be one flesh.
But he that is joined unto the Lord is one spirit.
Flee fornication. Every sin that a man (or woman) doeth is without the body; but he that committeth fornication sinneth against his own body. What? Know ye not that your body is the temple of the Holy Ghost which is in you, which ye have of God, and ye are not your own:
For ye are bought with a price; therefore glorify God in your body, and in your spirit which are God's" (1 Corinthians 6:15-20).

So much for, "I will do things my way; after all it's MY body." You see, it is not your body, it is God's.

"Dearly beloved, I beseech you as strangers and pilgrims abstain from fleshly lusts, which war against the soul" (1 Peter 2:11).

PART 3: SPIRITUAL WARFARE

You are a stranger and a pilgrim now since you have given your life to Christ. The more you change, the more you will realize that you are quite different than those who refuse to receive the wonderful Lord Jesus and what He has done to redeem us from our sin.

"Neither filthiness, nor foolish talking, nor jesting, which are not convenient: but rather giving of thanks.
For this ye know, that no whoremonger, nor unclean person, nor covetous man, who is an idolater, hath any inheritance in the Kingdom of Christ and of God.
Let no man deceive you with vain words; for because of these things cometh the wrath of God upon the children of disobedience.
Be not ye therefore partakers with them.
For ye were sometimes darkness, but now are ye light in the Lord; walk as children of light" (Ephesians 5:4-8).

Remember, we are aliens now that we have been saved by the grace of God and filled with His Holy Spirit. We are living alongside those who have not been saved. We are, indeed, resident foreigners, pilgrims, and strangers. The Apostle Peter opens one of his letters by referring to Christians this way. Christians, being strangers and aliens means that we are different in a culture that is hostile to God. But now, if you are incarcerated, not only are you living in a world that is hostile to God, but you are living in a culture that is hostile in many other ways as well. It won't be easy being a Christian in jail or prison, but you can be free on the inside no matter where you are and there are many on the outside who are in prisons much worse than the facility you are in, prisons of hopelessness.

Christians are Different

If we are different, then just exactly how are we different? Remember what we learned about Zoë life? We're different because we have hope. Zoë life gives us hope for the future and that hope for the future changes the way we see ourselves in the here and now. Yes, we are aliens here and that should affect the way we live from day to day. Because heaven is our home, hope for the future is the key to our identity as Christians.

Just what makes us different? We are different because, unlike those in the world, we are indwelled by the Holy Spirit of God with Zoë life. We are aliens in a foreign, pagan land until Jesus comes and takes us to our real homeland, heaven. We are no longer a part of the world system. We are living alongside of those who are hostile to God. Most of all we are different because we have hope for the future – not only for the future here on earth, but for our future in heaven. Hope is the great motivation in the Christian's life and hope is the reason that Christians endure suffering. The Apostle Peter says it is only for a little while until God takes us to heaven and it's worth it.

But, you might say, what about now? Jesus is there with you now. He is everywhere you are. He will never leave you or forsake you. King David prayed to God with a prayer of a believing heart. He wrote:

"Whither shall I go from thy spirit? Or whither shall I flee from thy presence?
If I ascend up into heaven, thou art there. If I make my bed in hell, behold, thou art there.

If I take the wings of the morning and dwell in the uttermost parts of the sea, even there shall thy hand lead me, and thy right hand shall hold me" (Psalms 139:7-10).

Then, in Psalm 144 King David goes on to say:

'Blessed be the Lord my strength, which teacheth my hands to war, and my fingers to fight" (Psalm 144:1).

But what are we to fight? We are to fight sin, temptation, and the works of the flesh, not one another. King David was called upon to wage war for himself and for the nation of Israel but we can apply this message to us today, believers in Christ, whom God has called to wage spiritual warfare against Satan, the world, and the flesh. We must press forward in Christ by proclaiming the gospel in the power of the Holy Spirit by bringing down Satan's strongholds, and by leading others to salvation in Christ.

CHAPTER **17**

Pulling Down Strongholds

The Weapons of our Warfare

THE LORD WANTS you to capture demonic strongholds, those areas of thinking that hold your mind in captivity. He wants to strengthen in you the stronghold of the Holy Spirit.

> *"For the weapons of our warfare are not carnal, but mighty through God to the pulling down of strongholds;*
> *Casting down imaginations, and every high thing that exalts itself against the knowledge of God, and bringing into captivity every thought to the obedience of Christ"* (2 Corinthians 10:4, 5).

Now these fighting words are metaphorical (symbolic). They are descriptions. They speak of weapons, strongholds, high things and bringing things into captivity. These are not carnal or worldly weapons, but spiritual ones.

The Bible is not referring to strongholds of stone but rather the strongholds of our imaginations. It's not referring to high things in high towers but it is referring to high-minded attitudes. It's not referring to taking into captivity enemy soldiers but enemy thoughts. The battlefield the Bible is referring to is the battle of the mind.

Let's look more closely at these metaphors and their figurative aspects. What is a stronghold? Why are strongholds important in literal warfare? Did you ever wonder about that? A stronghold is a defensive structure.

"The Lord also will be a refuge for the oppressed, a refuge in times of trouble" (Psalms 9:9).

The Hebrew word there is *misgav*; which means a cliff or other lofty or inaccessible place. It refers to a refuge – a defense, a high fort or tower. So a cliff could be a stronghold, because it's high and inaccessible to one's enemies.

In the book of 1 Samuel we see that David stayed in the desert strongholds and in the hills of the Desert of Ziph.

"And David abode in the wilderness in strongholds, and remained in a mountain in the wilderness of Ziph" (1 Samuel 23:14).

Why would someone live on a cliff in the wilderness when an enemy is in pursuit? Because it's safe up there! If an enemy comes, it's much easier to drive him away from a stronghold that is in a high place than it would be from a stronghold in a low place. You can learn about the strategic importance of strongholds in the history of wars where for years a stronghold threatened the security of a nation.

Think about it, how many years has a stronghold threatened your security in the heart of your thought life? Isn't it about time you went up there and captured it? It can be done you know! God knows all about your strongholds and He knows how to take them — and He will show you how to do it, if you are willing to fight. When you come up against something that seems to be a stronghold in your life, do you just want to give up? Or are you going to be willing to fight to take down that stronghold? Strongholds are captured by people who are willing to fight, people with courage!

A Stronghold is a Place or a Habitual Pattern

One thing you should bear in mind about a stronghold is that it is not a person, it is a place. A stronghold is only a threat if there are enemy soldiers inside. You see, a stronghold can also be a place of comfort, a safe place. It can be a rock, a fortress or a shield of protection. David was a man after God's heart. He knew that even if the enemy was nipping at his heals he could always depend upon God to hear him and come to his defense. Read this passage of Scripture and read it again and again whenever you feel the devil nipping at you.

"And David spake unto the Lord the words of this song in the day that the Lord had delivered him out of the hand of all his enemies, and out of the hand of Saul (who was trying to kill him).
And he said, The Lord is my rock, and my fortress, and my deliverer;
The God of my rock; in Him will I trust: He is my shield, and the horn of my salvation, my high tower, and my refuge, my savior, Thou savest me from violence.
I will call on the Lord, who is worthy to be praised: so shall I be saved from mine enemies.

> *When the waves of death compassed me, the floods of ungodly men made me afraid;*
>
> *The sorrows of hell compassed me about; the snares of death prevented me;*
>
> *In my distress I called upon the Lord and cried to my God: and He did hear my voice out of His temple, and my cry did enter into His ears"* (2 Samuel 22:1-7).

You need to understand that the person or persons inside the stronghold could be your enemies or they could be your friends. In a spiritual stronghold, there could be demons or there could be the Holy Spirit.

A spiritual stronghold could also be *a habitual pattern* built into one's thought life. Satan and his minions want to capture the minds of people because the mind is the citadel (fortress) of the soul. He knows that whoever or whatever controls the mind controls a very strategic place in a person's life. If you want the abundant life and peace that God promises then you must allow His Holy Spirit to capture the strongholds in your mind. The book of Romans tells us:

> *"For they that are after the flesh do mind the things of the flesh; but they that are after the Spirit the things of the Spirit.*
>
> *For to be carnally minded is death; but to be spiritually minded is life and peace.*
>
> *Because the carnal mind is enmity against God; for it is subject to the law of God, neither indeed can be.*
>
> *But ye are not in the flesh, but in the Spirit, if so be that the Spirit of God dwell in you. Now if any man have not the Spirit of Christ, he is none of His"* (Romans 8:5-9).

Two Kinds of People

In this portion of Scripture the Apostle Paul is describing two kinds of people; those who live according to the flesh, who desire to be occupied with the corrupt desires of sinfulness. Such living includes fornication, adultery, hatred, selfish ambition, outbursts of anger, obscenity, pornographic addiction, and drug addiction, mental and emotional pleasure from sex scenes in plays, book, TV, or movies, just to name a few. When the Bible refers to "the flesh" it is speaking about the sinful element of human nature, the part of you that wants to go along with the devil, the part of you that is always warring against you in your mind and body.

If you want the abundant life and peace that God has promised you then you must allow His Holy Spirit to capture those strongholds.

"For as he thinketh in his heart, so is he" (Proverbs 23:7).

Your mind and your thought life are not the only targets however. Even the words of your mouth can bring abundance or lack, blessing or cursing. Obscenity coming out of your mouth not only hurts the ones it is aimed at, it also will hurt you. The book of Matthew makes that clear.

O generation of vipers, how can ye, being evil, speak good things? For out of the abundance of the heart the mouth speaketh.

A good man out of the good treasure of the heart bringeth forth good things; and an evil man out of the evil treasure bringeth forth evil things.

> But I say unto you, that every idle word that men shall speak, they shall give account thereof in the Day of Judgment.
> For by thy words thou shalt be justified, and by thy words thou shalt be condemned" (Matthew 12:34-37).

A Stronghold Can be the Rut You Are In

Strongholds are also storage places, holding food, water and weapons. A stronghold gets stronger as more stuff—more thought—gets stored in it. In the life of the mind, the stuff that you were once aware of gets stored up in unconscious memory, and can make a stronghold difficult to take down. Be careful about what you think and what you store in your mind.

Sometimes a stronghold has become so much a part of a person that his or her way of thinking and feeling has developed a life of its own. It might be what is commonly referred to as a "rut." Perhaps it is a rut of depression or recurring unbelief or habitual bad temper. It might be a pattern of failure that keeps repeating itself: Sometimes a stronghold will cause you to provoke others to reject you without you even realizing it.

You might have a stronghold of resentment or worthlessness. If a child is sexually molested and or verbally abused, a stronghold of worthlessness may build up a stockpile of negative thoughts: "I'm guilty. Nobody could really love me. I'm good for nothing. I'm ugly." A girl might actually be beautiful — and certainly is beautiful in the eyes of God. But a stronghold gets filled with arguments like these: "Nobody would like me if they really got to know me. Nobody really knows me. Nobody really cares for me. Nobody is really interested in me for me."

Now all these thoughts may be a pack of lies, but they can

be a stronghold keeping out the truth of God's love. Such a person may hear a message about God's love, whether from a pulpit or a friend, but it goes in one ear and out the other, bouncing off the walls of a stronghold of rejection or worthlessness. You almost hear the truth come to set you free, and then along comes another thought, "Yeah, but what about...?" Or "You just don't understand...." And out comes another string of lies, excuses, and smokescreens.

So it is that a stronghold creates an inner captivity to deception and misery. A stronghold keeps a person from thinking clearly, accepting the truth, repenting of sin, and receiving deliverance. A stronghold can keep an unbeliever from hearing the Good News or the fullness of the Good News.

Taking Down a Stronghold

So how do you take down a stronghold? First, you have to recognize it, so you know what you're dealing with. It is difficult to take down a stronghold you can't even see, but strongholds of the mind can be hidden—evil things hang out in darkness. Satan is the prince of darkness, but Jesus is the Prince of light and you have been called out of darkness into His marvelous light!

"But ye are a chosen generation, a royal Priesthood, an holy nation; that ye should show forth the praises of Him who hath called you out of darkness into His marvelous light" (1 Peter 2:9).

Nevertheless, if there is an old, sinful pattern of thought in you, that sinful pattern of thought is a place of darkness and any place of darkness can be a stronghold.

"And have no fellowship with the unfruitful works of darkness, but rather reprove (disapprove of) them: (Ephesians 5:11).

If you want to let the light of God expose the darkness, you need an attitude of humility. You need to be willing to let the light of God reveal the darkness in you. Ask Him to shine the light of His Holy Spirit on those areas in your mind that have been in darkness to you.

David prayed, "Examine me, O Lord, and prove me; try my reins (what is in my mind) and my heart" (Psalm 26:2).

David was not a perfect man but he was a humble man. He admitted his failures to God. If you are not willing to pray like David did, then perhaps you need to tear down the stronghold of pride so that you, too, can come to God the Father in humility. Satan uses pride as armor so that he can keep demonic strongholds hidden. Pride keeps people from ever seeing that they are trapped in demonic darkness. The Spirit of God, however, is determined to bring down the stronghold of pride. If you allow God to work in your life, coming to Him in humility He will help you to bring down strongholds you have been struggling with for years.

"And the fortress of the high fort of thy walls shall He bring down, lay low, and bring to the ground, even to the dust" (Isaiah 25:12).

If pride is bad news, how much more is humility good news!

PART 3: SPIRITUAL WARFARE

"But He giveth more grace. Wherefore He saith, God resisteth the proud, but giveth grace unto the humble" (James 4:6).

This is a promise: humility releases grace, the power of God to save you.

"Submit yourselves therefore to God. Resist the devil, and he will flee from you.
"Draw nigh to God, and He will draw nigh to you. Cleanse your hands, ye sinners; and purify your hearts, ye double minded.
Be afflicted, and mourn, and weep; let your laughter be turned to mourning and your joy to heaviness.
"Humble yourselves in the sight of the Lord, and He shall lift you up" (James 4:7-10).

God loves humility and can work with the heart that is humble. We all need to understand how much God hates pride. It will cause God to turn away from our prayers and withhold His presence from us. When we are full of pride, what we are saying, in effect, is that we don't need God. Conversely, Satan can't stand humility! It breaks his power over you!

Once the Holy Spirit exposes an area of darkness, that is a stronghold in your life, the next step to bringing it down is repentance. Resist the temptation to defend yourself because if you do, you may never see what is wrong in you, or face what needs to change. You do not need to justify and defend yourself, instead, let God defend and justify you.

Stubborn Strongholds

Suppose a stronghold has gotten pretty entrenched and it seems nothing will budge it and pull it down. Successful military planners surround a stronghold and cut off its supplies. This strategy can also apply to spiritual strongholds. Surround that stronghold with the praises of God and cut off the supplies from the realm of darkness with all its negative thinking and bad, destructive habits.

Surround the stronghold with praise, singing psalms and spiritual songs to God. Demons can't stand praise! Praise is a powerful way to bring down a stronghold. For every negative stronghold, there's a powerful way to surround it with opposite truth from God.

If you are struggling with a stronghold of depression, surround it with hope. If you are struggling with a stronghold of rejection, surround it with acceptance. If you are struggling with a stronghold of unresolved anger, surround it with forgiveness. If you are struggling with a stronghold of fear, surround it with God's love and if you are struggling with a stronghold of failure, surround it with the victory of the resurrection! Once you have identified a stronghold, go to the Scriptures, and study the opposite truth from God's Word.

Following is a prayer for you. Pray it with all your heart.

Lord, please examine my heart and mind. Show me any areas in my life that I have not surrendered to you and have become strongholds Thank you Lord for cleansing me and making me whole from the inside out. I submit myself to the light of the Spirit of Truth to expose any strongholds, lies, deception, and sin in me. I want every stronghold in my life to

be brought down and I will surround them with praise. I ask you Lord to help me give up all patterns of negative thinking and purpose in my heart to think wholesome thoughts. I purpose in my heart to say wholesome words. I purpose in my heart to build up the stronghold of God in me. I pray this in Jesus name. Amen.

CHAPTER 18

Cutting the Cords to the Past

Mindsets

YOU MAY HAVE already figured out that some of our past is dictated by the generational patterns in our families. You just may not have known what to do about it, and thought you just had to live with it. God wants to mold us more and more into His image and get us out of those old patterns and mindsets. Some of those old mindsets say that whenever anything good happens to you then something bad will always follow. A mindset is a set of beliefs or a way of thinking that determines your behavior and outlook. For your behavior and outlook on life to change, your mindset must change.

What often happens when you get some kind of breakthrough in life is that the enemy comes in and robs your victory. He tells you that the opposite of the breakthrough is really true. Because Satan is telling you the opposite, it is usually how you can tell what God is really saying and what is really happening. Oh, you could NEVER DO THAT comes through loud and clear but the still small voice is saying, you can do all things through Christ.

"I can do all things through Christ which strengtheneth me" (Philippians 4:13).

"Do not grieve, for the joy of the Lord is your strength" (Nehemiah 8:10b).

When you're not sure what God is saying to you, ask yourself what the still, small voice is saying. The enemy speaks loud and clear and opposite of what God says. If the devil tells you that you will never get free, it is because the Lord is saying, you now know the truth and you **are** free.

"And after the earthquake; a fire but the Lord was not in the fire; and after the fire the still small voice" (1 Kings 19:12).

Don't let the devil get you down and depressed because all you have to do is walk out of the wilderness of lies. He wants you depressed because he knows that it is the joy of the Lord that is your strength. If you let Satan rob your joy, he's got your strength. **If we find our joy in Him, we can overcome any obstacle.** That is why we need to read the Bible because that is how we learn what the truth really is. You see, if we know the truth, it will set us free.

Identity Theft

Has the devil stolen your true identity? We need to know the truth about who we are, what our "true identity" is. Ask the Holy Spirit to reveal whatever is hindering you from realizing who you are in Christ. It could be a stronghold of fear that has been passed down generationally through the bloodlines of your family. It is pretty common knowledge that we inherit physical traits but few realize that we also inherit spiritual and emotional ones as well. This is what is referred to as a generational pattern. If it is a negative characteristic that we have inherited, and if it is a pattern that has repeated itself over and over again, it is called a generational curse. According to Scripture, generational curses (such as iniquity, illness, sins of the fathers) are passed to the third and fourth generation Sometimes even God's people are unable to move forward because of fear, intimidation and false identities.

We need to be seriously committed to breaking these old generational patterns and curses and move out of our past and into our future. We need to cut the cords to our past. We don't have to accept them. We can break them and stop them in their tracks.

Family Matters

Perhaps you are already getting a revelation of how you are connected to certain things that have run in patterns in your family. Maybe your father, your grandfather and great-grandfather were all alcoholics and addicted to riotous living. Maybe several members of your family committed suicide, were murdered, or died young, maybe more than a few are now, or have been incarcerated. In my family there were many drunks, and it seemed that in every generation there was the death of a baby. The Lord will bring to your mind the strongholds in your family that need to be dealt with.

Many of us, because of these patterns have felt as if we have been open prey to the enemy but God is teaching us that if we close the doors to the past by cutting our ties and cutting the umbilical cord to our past family behavior, and our past personal behavior then we can be free of these deadly strongholds that have been generational assignments meant to destroy us.

When you pray to God, pray against the devil. Inform him that you are cutting the cords to your past and moving on to God's plan for your life.

Discontentment

How many times I hear my great-grandchildren say, "I'm bored." Discontentment and boredom seem to be one of our human weaknesses. God, however, tells us that we are to be content with what we have.

> *"But Godliness with contentment is great gain.*
> *For we brought nothing into this world, and it is certain we can carry nothing out.*
> *And having food and raiment (clothing) let us be therewith content"* (1 Timothy 6:6-8).

There are two types of discontentment though, one spiritual and one carnal. One of the reasons we may have made such messes of our lives in the past is because we were so discontented. Most people in the world are discontented, frustrated, discouraged, and depressed and don't know where they fit in life. We are to be discontented with our spiritual condition to the point that we continue to strive for more of God, however, being discontent with life in general leads to misery and all kinds of sin. It is what kept Israel wandering in the wilderness for 40 years. If we allow a spirit of discontentment to keep us wandering in a spiritual wilderness trying to find contentment, we will never get out of the desert.

If you have given your heart to and surrendered your life

to Christ then you are part of the Body of Christ. Your identity is that you are a child of the Living God. If we look for contentment and acceptance elsewhere, we will continue to remain in the wilderness. Make a decision today, with an act of your will to accept the fact that you indeed are content in Christ. Make this decision with an act of your will whether you feel it or not. Eventually the Holy Spirit will give you contentment in your heart.

Satan desires to have us discontented. It is a way that he can exalt himself and his words above God's. He wants to destroy us and slay us by speaking lies to us and then getting us to speak lies to ourselves. If we believe what he says over what God says, we're in trouble! We need to cut that cord to the devil's lies; otherwise we will continue to be held captive by them.

Yet another thing that is the devil's job is to destroy our image. We are created in the image of God, not apes, and if the devil can seduce us to believe that we are merely animals who are unworthy, hopeless, and not measuring up, we are exalting Satan's words above what God has said concerning us. If we have an image of ourselves that is opposite of what God has declared, then we are bowing down to a false image and are in the sin of idolatry. We are never to bow down to a false image.

Time to Cut the Cord

In the natural, an umbilical cord is God's way of feeding an infant before birth. It is like a feeding tube that connects the baby to the mother so that the baby can be nourished while still in the womb, the entire nourishment for the baby is given through this cord. However, the cord is to be cut right after the delivery of the baby. In the spiritual realm, many of us have not cut the cord to the old feeding tube. We have listened to the enemy's lies and have been fed by our past wounds, behaviors and belief systems. A baby cannot survive in its new life if it is still connected to an old umbilical cord and likewise, we, as baby Christians cannot survive in our new born again life unless we cut the cord to those old wounds, behaviors and belief systems. God wants to begin to feed us from His word. When you leave the sin life behind you no longer need to be fed by sin. God wants to cut the cords to your past as well. He wants to feed, nourish, and care for you.

God desires to cover our nakedness with His love and power so that we can move away from barrenness and begin to grow and mature and begin to bear godly fruit. He desires to cleanse us, anoint us and wash us from our sinfulness. These are wonderful promises but we must be willing to receive them. If we are unwilling to receive God's full blessing in our lives it is this attitude that will keep us in bondage. We must choose to cut those cords to our past so that we can be free. Make a decision today to hear Him and move forward to fulfill your divine destiny. Get curious about moving into God's plan for your life. Ask Him to reveal it to you. You can pray this prayer:

Father, I seize this moment of opportunity for breakthrough in my life. I have been held captive long enough and I desire to live and move and have my being in You. I thank You that You have provided insight on how I can be set free. I cut the cords of my past, I cut off the source that has been feeding me the devil's lies and I ask that You begin to feed me Your truth. I break every assignment over me from the devil

and I decree and declare that I will no longer be hindered by my past. I make a decision to cut myself loose from the old past life. I will no longer listen to the lies of the devil. I thank You for the Holy Bible that is the Sword of the Spirit and that cuts me loose from my past. I confess that I am being cut free from all generational iniquities and patterns. I thank You that I am no longer held captive to barrenness and death. I will live and not die! In Jesus' name. Amen.

CHAPTER 19

Pharmakeia

Drug Abuse is Sorcery and Witchcraft

THE GREEK WORD pharmakeia in a positive context literally means to administer drugs but in the negative context it refers to the abuse of drugs. Drug abuse is closely associated with witchcraft and sorcery. Of course using drugs (medications) to make you well is not what is implied here but rather drug abuse. The problem is not non addictive medications that are legally prescribed for the purpose of treating disease. Drugs that give the users a high and or cause them to hallucinate and the drugs that cause users to enter into an altered state of consciousness are the problems. The Bible teaches that Christians are to be sober and of a sound mind yet we are stuck in a ridiculous cultural habit of thinking that medication will save us from every disease and will keep us from having to face reality.

Staying sober and maintaining a clear mind so as to stay out of the grasp of the devil should be reason enough to stay away from illegal drug use. Not only do we need to stay sober to maintain a clear mind, but abusing drugs causes demonization. Christians are not to use anything that will cloud their thinking or invite the devil into their lives. Alcohol, and some other drugs, for example, are intoxicating, but are also depressants that lower inhibitions and cause people to engage in behavior that is not pleasing to God. In the Bible, strong drink is associated with the works of the flesh, even fornication.

"*Their drink is rebellion, they commit harlotry continually. Her rulers dearly love dishonor*" (Hosea 4:18).

"*Woe to you who make your neighbors drink, who mix in your venom (adding herbs or drugs to wine) even to make them drunk so as to look on their nakedness (to seduce them)!*" (Habakkuk 2:15).

Works of the Flesh

"*Now the works of the flesh are manifest, which are these; adultery, fornication, uncleanness, lasciviousness.
Idolatry, witchcraft, hatred, variance, emulations, wrath, strife, seditions, heresies.
Envyings, murders, drunkenness, revellings, and such like; of the which I tell you before, as I have also told you in time past, that they which do such things shall not inherit the Kingdom of God*" (Galatians 5:19-21).

Those who abuse drugs are operating in the flesh and are much more likely to engage in sinful behavior. So that you will know what those old fashioned, King James, words mean I will spell them out for you. You need to know just exactly what the Bible refers to as the works of the flesh so that you can avoid them the best that you can.

Adultery: Sexual relations of a married person with someone other than his or her spouse.
Fornication: Immoral sexual conduct and intercourse; it includes taking pleasure in pornographic pictures, films, or writing.
Uncleanness: Sexual sins, evil deeds, and vices, including thoughts and desires of the heart.
Lasciviousness: Sensuality, following one's passions and desires to the point of having no shame or public decency.
Idolatry: Worship of spirits, persons, or graven images, also trust in any person, institution, or thing as having equal or greater authority than God and His Word.
Witchcraft: Sorcery, spiritism, black magic, worship of demons, and use of drugs to produce spiritual experiences.
Hatred: Intense, hostile intentions and acts, extreme dislike or enmity.
Variance: Quarreling, antagonism, a struggle for superiority.
Emulations: Resentfulness, envy of another's success.
Wrath: Explosive anger or rage which flares into violent words and deeds.
Strife: Selfish ambition and seeking of power.
Seditions: Introducing divisive teachings not supported by the Word of God.
Heresies: Division within the congregation into selfish groups or cliques, which destroy the unity of the church.
Envyings: Resentful dislike of another person who has something that one desires.
Murders: Killing a person unlawfully and with malice.
Drunkenness: Impairing one's mental or physical control by alcoholic drink or mind bending drugs.
Revellings: Excessive feasting, revelry, a party spirit involving alcohol, drugs, sex, or the like.

It couldn't be any clearer. Sin will not be tolerated by God and those who insist on remaining in its grip will not see the Kingdom of God.

Legalize Drugs?

There is a lot of arguing back and forth about legalizing drugs these days. One of the arguments is that we are losing the war on drugs anyway, so why not legalize them? Their argument is that after all the money that the government spends enforcing drug laws, it still continues. However, we can't stop chasing other crimes and criminals because we are losing the war on thieves or murderers. It is not the ability of drug laws to be enforced that is in question; rather it is the immorality of drug use, all the ruined lives, and crimes that are associated with it that matter. If the most abused drugs were made legal, they would still cost money; therefore the users would still lie, steal, and prostitute themselves to get them.

Some argue that drug use will continue no matter what, so we have to make it safer by handing out clean needles. This seems like a good idea, but it is encouraging drug use just like handing out birth control in schools is encouraging harmful sex practices among our children. Another argument is that we should not tell people what to do with their own bodies. The problem with that argument is that tobacco and marijuana are known carcinogens which end up costing the tax payers money for health care of the individuals who use. Drug abuse causes distortion in the senses. The perception of sight, sound, time, and touch is distorted. Thinking and problem solving are also interfered with and it can cause paranoia, anxiety attacks and loss of coordination. People who drive under the influence of drugs and alcohol are a main cause of the traffic accidents on our roads. So, you see, the reason drugs are illegal is because they are known to cause great harm, not only to the abuser but to society in general.

Why People Turn to Drugs

People who have a history of drug use, abuse, or addiction in their families are at higher risk for drug addiction themselves. It is a proven fact that kids of alcohol and drug-addicted parents and relatives are far more likely to have addictive tendencies than children of non-addicted family members. The kids of those addicted to alcohol or drug use see their parents abusing drugs to escape from their problems so when they encounter problems themselves they are more likely than other kids to look to drugs also since they have learned to think that drugs are a way to escape. The problem with this stinkin' thinkin' is that the reality they find in drugs trying to escape reality is a worse reality than the reality from which they were attempting to escape.

Sometimes though there is no sad family background story behind addiction. Often with an addiction to medically prescribed drugs, the dependent person started taking the prescription drugs because they were overcoming some type of surgery, legitimate disease or pain. Over time, however, they started to feel that they were incapable of living without their medication, and that if they stopped taking their prescription they would have to suffer the pain. There are, however, pain medications that are not addictive.

Then there are people with low self-esteem who may be more prone to drug addiction. Such persons may feel they have no have control over their lives and will turn to drugs as a way to cope. They often feel they can't please the people around them so they have to transform themselves in order to fit in. The change is made easier by abusing drugs because the artificial stimulants give them energy, motivation, and focus to make them into somebody and something that they are not. Stress is also one of the reasons for drug addiction. There again, the stress that is caused by the drugs is worse than the stress the person is trying to alleviate. When they discover that, however, it is too late, they are addicted.

Many single mothers, in an attempt to carry the entire burden of a family alone turn to stimulants. They are caring for the children alone, working a full time job, paying for child care, and keeping a home together by paying rent, buying groceries and all the responsibilities of homework and keeping involved with their children's schools and their education. Stimulants help them do it all and become "super moms" but in the process they get hooked.

Some of us are more able to cope with life than others. Some turn to drugs to help with anxiety. Once a person starts using drugs to overcome anxiety it can be hard to stop the cycle because the worries are still there once the high is gone, so the user feels he or she requires more drugs to bring more support. That type of cycle can also lead to long-term addiction.

One of the biggest reasons for the drug problems we see today is that drugs are very easily accessible. When I counsel former addicts and ask them where they got the drugs, the answer is always the same, "Drugs are everywhere!" You don't even need to have contact with neighborhood dealers anymore because illegal substances, alcohol and medically prescribed drugs really are "everywhere."

PART 3: SPIRITUAL WARFARE

The Drug Addiction Spectrum

Webster's dictionary definition of the word spectrum is "a continuous sequence or range." Drug addiction causes a sequence of events often referred to as a spectrum. Imagine a stone dropping in water where the effects of the stone drop fans out in all directions. One drug addict affects many people and society in general – moms, dads, husbands, wives, kids, other family members, friends, tax payers, medical and hospital costs, and the list goes on.

There are no easy answers to why people abuse drugs but the reasons can be put into some general categories. These are some of the reasons given by addicts and former addicts: They use to escape from the problems of life, from guilt, shame, or oppression of some kind. Drugs help relax, relieve boredom, pain, and help them to feel part of the "crowd." The many reasons given, however, are not valid reasons and people need to realize that life offers many other alternatives and better solutions to life's problems than taking drugs. These solutions, however, tend to take time and effort and these people usually want instant gratification instead.

Drug use is "magical thinking." This is thinking that is creating the illusion of power and control. It is about having feelings of mastery over life circumstances that make people feel weak and powerless. The problem is that it results in hopelessness. So why do people use drugs anyway? The easy answer is that people use drugs in order to have control over their moods, but the question as to why some people need so badly to have control over their moods while other people manage to cope without drugs, has no simple answer.

In interviewing some homeless people I discovered that a

large percentage of them turned to drugs, alcohol, and a life of homelessness because in one way or another they feel that they have been betrayed, let down or hurt by a person with whom they were in a relationship. They have used the drugs to insulate themselves against the suffering and pain caused by the rejection. However, the problem is that after awhile, drugs become less effective. It seems that first magnificent high can never again be recaptured. Everything about the drug culture eventually fails to live up to what it is originally cracked up to be. Consequently, more and more of the drug is needed just to continue to feel normal.

Drug addiction costs money and money to buy drugs becomes a problem because drug abuse causes job loss due to the addiction. As a result, crime becomes the only possible source of income. Relationships suffer and friendships are lost. Gradually, homes are also lost because they can no longer be afforded when every bit of money that is obtained goes toward buying more drugs. Filth, infection, theft and violence are all part of the drug spectrum as well.

What is Sorcery (Pharmakeia?)

The Bible equates drug abuse with sorcery. Sorcery is witchcraft and witchcraft is sin. It is the dependence on black arts and the supernatural instead of dependence on God. It is magic, enchantment, divination, calling upon evil spirits for assistance. It is voodoo, magic spells, Tarot card reading, psychic readings, séances, astrology, horoscopes, reincarnation, etc. You might say, "What's the harm in going to psychics and reading my horoscope? Well, let me tell you!

Many believe that since there is only one God, there can only be one source of the supernatural.

PART 3: SPIRITUAL WARFARE

"There is one body, and one Spirit, even as ye are called in one hope of your calling:
One Lord, one faith, one baptism,
One God and Father of all, who is above all, and through all, and in you all" (Ephesians 4:4-6).

There are, however, "spiritual forces of darkness"

"For we wrestle not against flesh and blood, but against principalities, against powers, against the rulers of darkness of this world, against spiritual wickedness in high places" (Ephesians 6:12).

The Bible makes it clear that we are to trust only in God and if we are putting our trust and confidence in Him, we have no reason to trust in the forces of darkness. At one time in my life I trusted in reading my horoscope and seeing what the stars were saying about my life. However, something miraculous happened when I became born again. It was then that I was able to trust in and consult with the One who created not only those stars, but the entire universe!

How are Drug Abuse and Sorcery Related?

Please understand that it is not a sin to take aspirin for a headache or antibiotics for infections. It is sinful, however, to use drugs for recreational purposes. Marijuana, Cocaine, Heroin, PCP, Methamphetamines, Crystal Meth, LSD, Ecstasy, Opium, and abuse of addictive prescription medications are what is in question here. These kinds of drugs, and their use, result in your becoming a slave to them and them becoming your idol rather than God being your Master. We need to avoid anything that becomes our idol and we need to avoid recreational drug use. Medicine is one thing but drug abuse is quite another!

The Plague of OxyContin and Roxicodone

One of the most abused drugs on the market today is OxyContin. Roxicodone is a brand name and is the instant release form of the opiate as opposed to the extended time release OxyContin. Its use and abuse is pandemic. It is a new pain medicine with terrible side effects. This drug contains a powerful alkaloid that is derived from opium. OxyContin is becoming the new drug of choice in America and has replaced cocaine, heroin, and ecstasy as the number one killer in some states. Just the pain killing effects of the opium are experienced, with these drugs, not the mind altering effects I estimate that nearly 100 percent of the women I counsel in our county jail have been addicted to these drugs. Many are there because of OxyContin addiction and the felonies they have committed associated with the addiction. They have committed crimes in order to support their habits such as breaking and entering, shoplifting, forgery, stealing checks, extortion, and prostitution.

It all boils down to the fact that people today are worshipping self. They are self-centered and self-absorbed. Drug abuse is a quest for self-absorbed pleasure. It is another one of the devil's ways of bringing people under physical, psychological, psychosocial, and spiritual bondage.

Take the Jesus High Road

In the search for God, many people take the road that is

PART 3: SPIRITUAL WARFARE

broad that leads to destruction but we are to enter in at the strait gate, the narrow one that leads to God.

> "Enter ye in at the strait gate: for wide is the gate, and broad is the way that leadeth to destruction, and many there be which go in thereat" (Matthew 7:13).

That broad road is a search for an "experience" rather than submission to God. They that enter in are seeking feelings, rather than faith and when they can't find the feelings they are seeking they turn to drugs. A combination of drugs and the spiritual is a lethal combination and is the most dangerous kind of sorcery because it dulls the senses and creates a god in man's image, not man in God's image. It is a false god – SELF.

Pharmakeia is the ultimate sorcery because it uses mind-altering drugs in a search for God and it replaces God with the devil's lies. Sorcery is witchcraft, idolatry and blasphemy at its worst. You would think that with all the knowledge we have today regarding the dangers of drug abuse that people would stop looking for feelings, emotions, euphoria, or God in a pill.

God does not warn us of the dangers of inebriation to take away our fun or keep us from having a divine experience. These warnings are designed to protect us and remind us that we must be watchful that we do not fall into the hands of the devil. The devil will give you an experience alright, one that you will surely regret.

When the negative, unrighteous, thoughts come into your mind, rebuke them, and command them to leave you. You do not have to put up with thinking about getting high or getting back at someone. You can get so high on Jesus that you will never want to go back to drugs again. Drug addiction is a counterfeit of the high that Jesus gives. His high gives you a hang on, not a hangover and when you want more, you don't have to steal or prostitute your body to get it, all you have to do is call out to God and you will find that He is there with you all the time.

I have been privileged to have ministered to some girls who are very creative and have written poems about their addiction and their subsequent deliverance. They are speaking out of the core of their beings and I hope the words they speak will enter your heart and touch you in a mighty way.

Kitty, at this writing, is still in jail, but because of the relationship she has with the Lord, she is freer today in jail than she was on the street addicted to drugs.

Too Young To Die
By KR

I never thought I'd realize
   how lonely life could be.
I never thought the day would come
   when I'd get tired of me.
My voice was never softer
   than the day I said good-bye
To all the wild activities
   that helped to keep me high.
As I searched for some serenity
   I looked up toward the sky.
I prayed dear Lord please give me strength
   'cause I'm too young to die.

PART 3: SPIRITUAL WARFARE

If I knew then what I know now
    so much I could have been;
Instead I wasted cash and time
    on pills, cocaine, and gin.
So many truly wondrous things
    this world of ours contains.
When pondering the choices made
    I'm filled with guilt and shame.
How sorrowful I feel inside
    of wasted days gone by.
But thank the Lord I see today
    that I'm too young to die.

There are oh so many roads to travel,
    which path do I take?
When I look back upon my past
    it's clear I made mistakes.
Another mistake I can't afford,
    one more could cost my life!
When I think of all the games I played
    my conscience cuts deep as a knife.
It's a wonder I've a conscience at all
    after oh so many lies.
I need to make a change, and now,
    'cause I'm too young to die.

The sound of glasses toasting,
    that smoke I oh so crave,
The stinkin' smell of all that's hell,
    just look it's here to stay.
Do I run and hide, jump and die
    or allow myself to fall?

Should I harden my heart, tear it apart,
    or build a tall strong wall?
If you ask me why I chose the Lord
    I'll answer with a sigh.
Salvation is the only way
    'cause I'm too young to die!

Don't Use Cocaine My Friend
By KR

Don't ever use cocaine my friend
    You see, it never pays.
Although it causes broken lives
    It happens every day.
You wonder how to score each night
    You wonder what is true.
One moment you'll be happy,
    Next moment you'll be blue.
And then it starts, you don't know why
    But you need it night and day.
You see, my friend, you're losing it.
    It always ends this way.
Coke kills the pain that hurts too much
    But the price you pay is high.
If I had to choose between coke and death
    I think I'd rather die.
So, don't ever use cocaine my friend
    You'll be hurt before it's through.
You see my friend, I ought to know
    'cause I was a coke head too.

PART 3: SPIRITUAL WARFARE

Then there is Sarah, who after being raised in a godly home went out into the world and became addicted to Roxicodone and many other drugs as well. As a result she spent several months in jail. Drug addiction has no mercy. It is an equal opportunity detroyer. Addiction does not discriminate; it does not care if you are rich or poor, famous or unknown, a man or a woman, a Christian or an Atheist, or even if you are a child. It casts a long shadow. a shadow of death.

As Sarah's letters indicate, she has turned her back on drug addiction and jail for good. We never gave up on her. We prayed and cried out to God to keep her alive long enough to get her back from the hands of the devil. During this time the Lord gave me two words for her. He said, **"She will."** We clung to those words and believed God for a miracle. I am happy to tell you that she is free today, back with her children, and serving the Lord with all her heart.

Sarah finally agreed to enter Caring People Recover Center in Bowling Green, Florida. It changed her life! I highly recommend this ministry. Contact information for them can be found on the reference page at the end of the book. As a part of her recovery she was wisely instructed to write letters to her drug of choice, Roxicodone (Roxanne is its street name) and to her family members asking for forgiveness. As you read these letters I pray that they will cause you to examine your heart as she did hers.

Roxanne
By SL

Roxanne,
I'm writing this letter to say all of the things that have long needed to be said. I'm writing this to let you know that I am an-

gry with you, absolutely furious. You lied to me and made me believe that you were an angel that would take away my pain but instead you were a demon who came to control my life.

You left me, not only angry, but violent, cold-hearted, hopeless, helpless, and careless. Then you continued to send me further down the road to destruction. You filled my life with misery, sorrow, grief, and complete torment. You filled me with rage and hatred and turned me into a selfish, cold, irritable, self-loathing, ignorant, and foolish whore.

You stole my family's time, my children's time, my house, my cars, my driver's license, and my mind. You brought me to a point where I stole to get you and sold my body to feed your hunger and cravings. Most importantly, you robbed my soul and left me a hollow shell, merely existing in this world.

Then you brought me to a point where I injected you into my veins to numb myself from the inside out. You left me captive to your enslavement. You stole my dreams and my ambitions and made me believe I could do nothing and be no one. You stole my mother's daughter, my father's daughter, my grandmother's granddaughter, my brother's sister. I hate you, you venomous, selfish, relentless whore. You are driving my generation to lose their lives, their homes, and their families.

I'm saying goodbye to you for the last time Roxanne, goodbye to the stealing, to the making of bad decisions, and to the one dimensional thinking. Goodbye to spoons, needles, scars and scabs that left me empty and bleeding, not only on the inside but bloody on the outside as well. I'm saying goodbye to the cravings, the hot and cold sweats I suffered when I didn't answer your relentless knocking. Goodbye to vomiting and diarrhea. You left me too thin, sucked in, eaten up and starved. I will never give in to you again!

Goodbye Roxanne to the hopeless, helpless, careless, and

selfish, Godless faithless, shell I had become. Goodbye to the sex I had to get you and the manipulation and lies. Goodbye to the heartless, soulless, tormented, evil, cold-hearted, vengeful, angry, and beaten up, walked all over door mat that you turned me into.

Goodbye to the street life, the drug dealing, the prostitution. Goodbye to arrests, the cop car rides to jail, sally ports, handcuffs, shackles, courtrooms, black and white stripes, and living within the revolving doors of the Justice System – the probation, probation officers, urine screens. Goodbye to jail sentences, judges, pleas, liens, and the enslavement of it all. Goodbye to living with the feeling of living life from the inside looking out. Goodbye to correction officers, and 6' x 6' jail cells. Goodbye to the years you took from my babies. Goodbye to looking at my children and my family through glass after they had to go through metal detectors. Goodbye to rolling wire fences, cold jail cell bars, cold, hard brick walls that held my soul captive. You selfish whore, where were you then?

I have my family back now, my soul back, my life, my ambitions and dreams. You will never take so much as a day from my life or my children's lives again. Goodbye you God forsaken whore, goodbye!

Dear SL,

The time has come for you to forgive yourself for the years of your addition. I am asking you to forgive yourself for all of the self-induced drug use, the lying, the stealing, and the hopeless, helpless, controlling rages. To forgive yourself for the cold-hearted, hateful, numb, useless, vengeful and hollow shell you merely existed in. I am asking you to forgive yourself for the missed time, the birthdays, holidays with family, and the missed time with your children due to your being incarcerated.

Please forgive yourself for losing your soul to addiction, the endless chase to get drugs, the torment, the violent, lazy, Godless, faithless, heartless woman and mother you grew to be. Please forgive yourself for the envious, greedy, miserable, bleeding soul you allowed yourself to become. Please forgive yourself for running in the street life, for drug dealing, and the drug environment you lived in. Forgive yourself for being too thin, sucked in, eaten up. Forgive yourself for the craving, and for the starved, unambitious, dreamless, woman that you had become.

Forgive yourself, Sarah, for the arrests, the sentences, the jail time. Forgive yourself for the enslavement, the entrapment, of the 6' x 6' jail cells, and the inhuman existence you lived in. Forgive yourself for the sex to get drugs, for selling yourself and other young women to get drugs. Forgive yourself for the pornography, and sexual perversion. Forgive yourself for losing your children, your home, your jobs, your family and your very soul.

Please forgive yourself for shooting up, and giving up on yourself and for not loving yourself. Forgive yourself for taunting death day after day and merely existing in the pit of hell. Forgive yourself, Sarah, for giving up so quickly on your marriage, your children, and your family. Forgive yourself for being led down the path of destruction, for being used up, bottled up, shot up, scarred up, and for being the frightened, selfish, money driven whore you became. Please forgive yourself, Sarah, for all the hurt and pain you caused.

Love, SL

"Be sober, be vigilant; because your adversary the devil, as a roaring lion, walketh about seeking whom he may devour" (1 Peter 5:8).

CHAPTER **20**

Blessings Keep Devils Away

The Blessing of Obedience

THE BIBLE TEACHES volumes about blessings. Even the Old Testament, although it was written thousands of years ago, can speak to us today. God spoke a blessing over Abraham in the Old Testament but that blessing affects every Christian today. Everything in the Garden of Eden was available to Adam and Eve if they did one thing – obey God. When they disobeyed, however, a great curse came upon all mankind to every color, nation, and religion, for all time. We have carried on the disobedient behavior in our own lives generation after generation. Disobeying God's Word will always bring curses but obeying His word will, without fail, brings blessings into our lives. It is always God's will that we be blessed. Redemption was God's answer for breaking the curses of disobedience; that's why Jesus came.

Even we, as born again Christians, cannot willfully disobey God and expect that curses will not fall upon us. Curses are the consequence of transgressions, iniquity, and sin. Blessings are the consequence of obedience. We as Christians must do our very best to walk as Jesus walked. God knew that we would not be able to obey Him to the fullest. That is why He so graciously provided a way to break the curses on our lives through Jesus Christ, and live blessed lives instead. There are, however, conditions that must be met.

The Blessing of Humility

"If we confess our sins, He is faithful and just to forgive us our sins, and to cleanse us from all unrighteousness.
If we say that we have not sinned, we make Him a liar, and His Word is not in us" (1 John 1:9, 10).

All of God's promises are blessings. When we are not seeing blessings operating in our lives we need to seek Him in humility to find out why. God wants to bless us because when we have God's fullness and blessings in our lives we can be Christians who demonstrate to others what God can and will do. This is the way in which we are able to attract those who need Jesus. Oh, they will see that Christians still have struggles, but the way in which we approach those struggles and deal with them is different. We have joy and it is the joy of the Lord that is our strength to get us through those struggles.

The Blessing of Joy

The joy of the Lord is our strength, if we let Satan rob our joy, we become weak and he can walk all over us.

"Then he said unto them, go your way, eat the fat, and drink the sweet, and send portions unto them for whom nothing is prepared; for this day is holy unto our Lord; neither be

ye sorry; for the joy of the Lord is your strength" (Nehemiah 8:10).

Before we turn our life over to God and are born again we walk under the law of sin and death but after we belong to Jesus, we are under the blood that Jesus Christ shed for us on the cross. He gave His life on that cross so that you and I could be free. He actually took the curse for us and gave us blessings instead. It is the blessings of God that bring joy.

"For the law of the Spirit of life in Christ Jesus hath made me free from the law of sin and death" (Romans 8:2).

"Christ hath redeemed us from the curse of the law, being made a curse for us: for it is written, Cursed is every one that hangeth on a tree:

That the blessing of Abraham might come on the Gentiles through Jesus Christ; that we might receive the promise of the Spirit through faith" (Galatians 3:13-14).

The Blessing of Hope

What great news! We deserve hell, and that is where we are headed until we receive Jesus. When we come to Him we get to spend eternity in heaven instead, what hope this brings us. That's not all though, we also are no longer under the curse of sin and sickness and now we have power over sin through Jesus Christ and having power over sin means that we have power over curses as well. However, we must want to overcome all the sin in our lives because if we want to keep on sinning we have no power to overcome.

Mark Driscoll in his book, Death by Love: Letters from the Cross, wrote:

> "The great Protestant Reformer Martin Luther rightly declares that at the moment Jesus became the most grotesque, ugly, and hideous thing in the history of all creation. In what Luther calls "the great exchange," the sinless Jesus so thoroughly took our place that He became the worst of what we are – rapists, thieves, perverts, addicts, liars, gluttons, gossips, murderers, adulterers, fornicators, homosexuals, and idolaters. Importantly, Jesus' work on the cross was not just a bookkeeping transaction in the divine economy. Jesus actually took to Himself our sin with all its horror and shame."

Pretty powerful, wouldn't you say? Breaking the curses over your life, however, involves acknowledging them and having a willingness to give them to God. You cannot overcome something you refuse to acknowledge and you cannot get rid of something you refuse to give up. You must repent for whatever involvement you had in the enemy's territory and that doesn't only mean asking forgiveness. It also means turning your back on that sin determining never to return to it again. Rebuke the devil in that area and command him to let go of you. Remind him that you no longer belong to him, but you now belong to the Lord Jesus Christ and remember "the great exchange." You give God your sin and He gives you His holiness and His righteousness. What a bargain!

The Blessing of Faith

In reading the Old Testament you will discover many

references to the blessings given to Abraham that include his seed, but who are Abraham's seed (his descendants?) In the book of Matthew we read:

"The book of the generations of Jesus Christ, the son of David, the son of Abraham" (Matthew 1:1).

This establishes Jesus as a seed of Abraham. We, who are born again, are brothers and sisters of Jesus so therefore, we are now the spiritual seed of Abraham as well. That means we are entitled to all of Abraham's blessings. God called Abraham Abram before he had the Holy Spirit on him. After that the ending of his name was like the breath of God.

God blessed Abram as He sends him out to a new country away from all his people. God did not tell Abram where He was sending him; only that He would show it to him as he went.

"Now the LORD had said unto Abram, Get thee out of thy country, and from thy kindred, and from thy father's house, unto a land that I will show thee:
And I will make of thee a great nation, and I will bless thee and make thy name great; and thou shalt be a blessing:
And I will bless them that bless thee, and curse them that curseth thee: and in thee shall all families of the earth be blessed" (Genesis 12:1-3).

"For when God made promise to Abraham, because He could swear by no greater, He swore by Himself, saying, surely blessing I will bless thee, and multiplying I will multiply thee" (Hebrews 6:13,14).

In the book of Ephesians the Apostle Paul begins his letter by listing the spiritual blessings we have in Christ. Notice how he begins by describing these blessings as spiritual blessings that are in heavenly places. This probably means that the real, true blessings are not physical or material.

"Blessed be the God and father of our Lord Jesus Christ, who hath blessed us with all spiritual blessings in heavenly places in Christ;

According as He hath chosen us in Him before the foundation of the world, that we should be holy and without blame before Him in love.

Having predestinated us unto the adoption of children by Jesus Christ to Himself, according to the good pleasure of His will.

To the praise of the glory of His grace, wherein **He hath made us accepted in the beloved.**

In whom we have redemption through His blood, the forgiveness of sins, according to the riches of His grace;

Wherein He hath abounded toward us in all wisdom and prudence;

Having made known unto us the mystery of His will, according to His good pleasure which He hath purposed in Himself" (Ephesians 1:3-9).

The Blessing of Adoption

Accepted in the Beloved? So much for rejection! This establishes it – the fact that we are Christ's and that we are accepted by Him and related to Him by adoption. We are part of the family of God, just as Abraham, David and Jesus were. Because we are His adopted children, we also have been given all spiritual blessings through the new birth purchased for us by Jesus Christ. We who are born again are spiritually the 'seed of Abraham' and are entitled to the full benefits of that promise that God made to him.

So, what does all this mean? It means that our sinful nature made us enemies of God and slaves to sin. God, however, has adopted us. Adoption allows non biological children all the privileges of a natural born child. We are not God's children naturally, but because of the forgiveness of God and the redemption He gives us we become His adopted children and because we are God's adopted children we are also heirs of everything He owns, and He owns everything!

We must know what the promised blessings are, however, and how we obtain them. This can only happen as we are obedient to God. We must pray that the eyes of our understanding be opened so that we can see the greatness of this covenant that He made with Abraham which also includes us. As we gain understanding of the precious provision this covenant gives us, then we need to make a decision to walk it out in our lives.

"That in the dispensation of the fullness of times He might gather together in one all things in Christ both which are in heaven and which are on earth, even in Him;

In whom also we have obtained an inheritance, being predestinated according to the purpose of Him who worketh all things after the counsel of His own will;

That we should be to the praise of His glory, who first trust in Christ.

In whom ye also trusted, after that ye heard the Word of truth, the gospel of your salvation;

In whom also after that ye believed, ye were sealed with

that Holy Spirit of promise which is the earnest (the down payment) of our inheritance until the redemption of the purchased possession, unto the praise of His glory" (Ephesians 1:3-14).

The Blessing of Peace

"For He is our peace, who hath made both one, and hath broken down the middle wall of partition between us" (Ephesians 2:14).

"I will both lay me down in peace, and sleep: for thou, Lord only makest me dwell in safety" (Psalms 4:8).

"Thou wilt keep him in perfect peace, whose mind is stayed on Thee: because he trusteth in Thee" (Isaiah 26:3).

"And the peace of God, which passeth all understanding, shall keep your hearts and minds through Christ Jesus" (Philippians 4:7).

"Now the Lord of peace Himself give you peace always by all means. The Lord be with you all" (2 Thessalonians 3:16).

It is easy to see by these passages of Scripture that the blessings that God has for us are blessings of hope, peace, well being, and abundant life. These are much better than blessings of money or power. However, make no mistake about it God's blessings do provide for our physical needs and desires as well. God the Father grants these blessings "in Christ." This is a continual theme we will see throughout the Bible.

PART 3: SPIRITUAL WARFARE

These portions of Scripture are by no means the only ones that pertain to peace. Look them up in the Concordance in the back of your Bible. If your Bible doesn't have one, then find one that does. It is an important tool. Here are some of the other blessings we have when we are "in Christ" and are Christians.

Blessings of love, comfort, contentment, courage, eternal life, faithfulness, fear of God, forgiveness, fruitfulness, grace, guidance, help in trouble, the Holy Spirit, honesty, long life, brotherly love, mercy, patience, prayer, trust, protection, righteousness, and wisdom. Freedom from worry and anxiety, freedom to worship and freedom from hell.

It becomes well with our soul when we choose the Lord Jesus Christ over life without Him.

CHAPTER **21**

Redeemed From the Curse

You are Redeemed From the Curse

WHEN I TURNED my life over to Jesus it was no surprise for me to learn that I had curses operating in my life. I learned that I was under the curse of the Law of God. My life was a disastrous mess! But I was very relieved, entering into deliverance counseling, a few weeks after getting saved, to learn that I was not the only one responsible for the chaos I had made of my life. I learned that I had been in bondage and that the voices in my head were evil spirits – actually entities like people without bodies in the spirit world who had been partially controlling my life and the lives of my family members for generations.

I realized that it was I who was responsible because of my own personal sin, but now I was learning about familiar spirits and their function in a person's life. You may have heard of them but not known what they were. They are evil spirits who are assigned to your family and are familiar with every aspect of your family's history for several generations before you were ever born. Their job is to pass on curses to as many generations as possible. Since they already have an inroad into a family, demon spirits are able to come in with their temptations and since they already know the weaknesses that exist in the family members, they know the very areas in which you will be vulnerable. These spirits can cause mayhem in a family for generations if they are not bound and cast out.

"*Keeping mercy for thousands, forgiving iniquity and transgression and sin, and that will by no means clear the guilty; visiting the iniquity of the fathers upon the children, and upon the children's children, unto the third and the fourth generation*" (Exodus 34:7).

Demons Must Have Permission

There is good news though. The good news is that demonic spirits do not have a right to you at any time. They must have permission before they can attack, harass, and torment you. Curses can only take effect in your life when you give them permission by personally committing sin. Only sin opens the door for the enemy to demonically bind you and not every curse your ancestors have committed opens the door. However, the familiar spirits will tempt you to commit the same sins your ancestors had problems with to get you to open the door for a curse to come on you.

This is why God is so adamant about your not sinning. It is not because He wants to spoil your fun; it is because He wants you to be safe. As an earthly parent you will protect your child from playing in the street because you know the child will be in danger of being hit by a car. Then how much more would your heavenly Father protect you from doing things that He knows will hurt you.

PART 3: SPIRITUAL WARFARE

"As the bird by wandering, as the swallow by flying, so the curse causeless shall not come" (Proverbs 26:2).

Generational Curses

But why would God punish three to four generations of ancestors with the sins of their fathers? Perhaps it is because of the degree to which God hates sin. When you know that your children are going to suffer for your sin, it makes sin a lot harder to commit. You know that children are the ones who pay the price for their parent's divorce, for alcoholism and abuse, etc. Obviously, generational curses are alive and well in the lives of those who are outside the new covenant with God (non-believers).

Some sins of your ancestors can attach themselves to you in the womb at conception. When that happens, you enter life with some demonic trait or weakness. Through deliverance and repentance you can break any curses that are on you. But you can see from Proverbs 26:2, above, that a curse can't land on you unless it has a cause. Unfortunately we give the devil plenty of cause with personal sins of our own!

Generational curses are judgments that are passed on to individuals because of sins that have been perpetuated in a family over a number of generations. Even doctors realize that generational curses exist. Unless they are Holy Spirit filled believers they just don't comprehend the spiritual implications. They only know that it happens and they blame it all on DNA and think it is all genetic. What is the first thing they ask you? What are the conditions, disorders, and diseases that your family members have had? They ask these questions because they know that these things can be passed on to you.

Generational curses are similar to original sin curses

because they can be passed down on a generational basis. They are different, however, because generational curses do not carry with them eternal judgment the way our personal sin of rejecting the Lord Jesus Christ can. In other words, generational sin curses won't necessarily land you in hell. Rather they bring the judgment or bondage during an individual's life, lessening his or her quality of life. They are temporary. They can cause a lot of grief, and they can make your life miserable, but they can be changed and they can be broken. One way to look at curses is that they get our attention and encourage us to turn back to God. That is exactly why God allows them. Those who are humbled by them will repent and find the Lord and restoration for their lives but those who become angry, bitter, rebellious, self-righteous and unrepentant go deeper into bondage and darkness and the curse is allowed to continue on in your family. It continues on to your children, grandchildren, and great grandchildren. The pattern will continue until someone addresses the sin issues that put the curses into operation in the first place.

Emotional and Spiritual Weaknesses

We all have emotional and spiritual weaknesses and because familiar (family) spirits have been in and around your family for a long time, they know just exactly what those weaknesses are. Nobody inherits all the family curses but because the devil knows what they are and what your weaknesses are that is where he will attack you.

It is amazing how creative the devil can be. For instance: You might think that because you hate the taste of alcoholic beverages and never became an alcoholic that you escaped a curse of alcoholism in your family and you are home free but because the curse of addition is present and the devil knows he can't tempt you with alcoholism, he might tempt you with drugs instead. You begin to use them and discover they will anesthetize you just as well, if not better than liquor and you don't need to taste them, just take pills, snort them into your nose or inject them into your veins. The devil doesn't care what your drug of choice is, just as long as he can get you to use. The next thing you know, you are hooked!

Maybe a few people in your family committed suicide. Well, you wouldn't think of doing such a thing but, you get drunk and drive your motorcycle like a maniac without a helmet and get into an accident and nearly die. Maybe it wasn't just an accident – maybe it was that self-destructive spirit of suicide that was subconsciously at work in you. The devil knows you don't have the guts to hang yourself, but he has no trouble trying to kill you while you are having fun on your motorcycle.

How do curses take away the quality of life? They can bring failure, shame, sickness and even physical death. Perhaps you have observed a father with a problem with rage and his son has the same problem. I have seen families where several members suffer from anxiety and depression. Many people are living with bondages that have been brought on by the generations that preceded them.

"Our fathers have sinned, and are not; and we have borne (been punished for) their iniquities" (Lamentations 5:7).

Look for Family Patterns

You can see that some symptoms of a generational curse are when there is a continual negative pattern of something being handed down from generation to generation. A good example is that often people who are adopted end up with the same characteristics as their birth parents. Even though they were not even raised with their birth parents they inherited their spiritual bondages. Some common symptoms of generational curses are family illnesses that seem to just go from one person down to the next (cancer is a common physical manifestation that can be from a spiritual bondage), continual financial difficulties (people continually hitting barriers in their finances), mental health problems, persistent irrational fears and depression. Anything that seems to be a continual struggle or problem that was handed down from one generation to another may very well be a generational curse. We all know that we inherit physically but few realize that we inherit spiritually as well.

The curses that are not necessarily generational but are brought on by our own foolish behavior are curses of disobedience. Before you became children of God and were born again Christians you had no choice but to suffer the effects of curses because of disobedience, but now that you are in the Lord, the choice to live in obedience to God is yours.

Reverse Those Patterns, Break Those Curses

You can break curses, reverse those patterns and turn them around. How do I do that you might be asking? The Scriptures reveal a two step approach for dealing with generational curses and the ones you brought on yourself. The first thing you must do is address your own personal sins, and then you can address the generational sins in your family. At this point, many Christians will reason, "I thought that all the past is under the blood when I received Jesus as my

PART 3: SPIRITUAL WARFARE

Savior!" That's like saying; "I thought the infection was gone, now that I have put a bandage on it." As far as your salvation and eternal destiny is concerned, that is true, but Satan loves to cause us grief when there is sin connected to our lives and when there is personal or generational, sin that has not been addressed through repentance and confession.

Remember that when you received Jesus into your life and you acknowledged your sin in a general way and asked Him to be your Savior and forgive you and cleanse you? The Lord was very gracious with your general confession, but later on the Holy Spirit began to convict you of sins in your past. You were led to repent of them and confess them specifically to the Lord. Why did the Holy Spirit do that? He did that because He wanted you to be free of any legal claims the enemy had on your life. It had nothing to do with your salvation, but it had a lot to do with the quality and freedom of your new life in Christ. It's called deliverance.

God doesn't cause curses or satanic hindrances but He will use the ones that are already at work in our lives to accomplish something good. These hindrances often give us the motivation to pursue a more sanctified and holy life.

Okay, so how do we begin to address the problem of generational curses and our own sin bondages? You can begin by making two sin lists - one personal and one for your family. Include your parents and the members of each of their families, your aunts, uncles, grandparents. Your personal list will probably be pretty easy because you are well aware of what you have done wrong but you will probably have to pray about your family list. The Holy Spirit will help you.

Start thinking about the stories you heard as a child about various people in the family. To put my family list together I began to recall seeing photographs of people I didn't even know who were distant cousins, uncles, aunts, etc. I remember my family members pointing to pictures and saying things like: "Yeh, these crazy Germans were some beer guzzlers alright. He was a drunk, and so was he, and his kid was a drunk too. They were some real rabble rousers alright." So now I had identified alcoholism, addiction, drunkenness, and even rabble rousing and carousing (riotous behavior). I noticed that every woman in my mother's family, although they weren't alcoholics, married drunks and had miserable marriages. My dad wasn't an alcoholic when my mother married him, but he did drink, and over the years he became one. Their marriage was miserable. So, now I was getting somewhere. Miserable marriages, marriage to drunks and alcoholics, and yes, I, too, married an alcoholic and had a miserable marriage. Oh, yes, and my brother was a drunk too.

After some digging I discovered that there had been several instances of infant deaths in my mother's family; stories of babies dying shortly before or after birth. Several of my cousins had babies who died. A couple of my aunts had babies who died. My mother's baby boy died at 4 months old, and, my forth baby, a baby boy I named Mark, was stillborn at full term. Are you starting to get the picture? I came against the curse of infanticide, dead babies and determined that the curse was not going into another generation!

Still another instance of a pattern was the witchcraft in both sides of my family. My mother said she was the "black sheep" of the family and they called her the "hex." Webster's Dictionary defines "hex" as a witch, a sign, a spell supposed to bring bad luck, a jinx. It's the number 6. So, when the Holy Spirit brought this back to my mind, I could see that there was a curse of witchcraft in my mother's family and a spell of bad things happening. She certainly had a life full of curses, her miserable marriage, a dead baby, five major surgeries, one of which nearly took her life, and cancer which did cause her death at the young age of 57. There's more in my mother's family, but let's go on to my father's family.

Generational Witchcraft

My father's nickname for me was "Bugaboo" which I later learned means evil spirit. I had been called an evil spirit from the time I was born! My father's mother, and her mother before her, were both alcoholics and I was not surprised to learn that they were also both "psychics." My father would tell me stories of how they would know things before they happened. Well, not only did I know psychically that my baby would die from the time I conceived him, but I had many psychic phenomena happen to me from the time I was a child. This was a witchcraft curse in operation that continued to get more powerful as the years went by. You see, because of this curse on me from before I was born, my spirit was wide open to this type of phenomena.

In my testimony I described how the devil lured me in through these "psychic" experiences and made me think I was someone special who had been "called" by God to be a witch. Most people do not know, and I certainly didn't, that there are two sources of the supernatural, one God and the other Satan. I thought the entire supernatural realm was of God. So, when my mother died, that is when I dove, head first into the devil's camp by trying to channel her spirit. What a big mistake that was!

The Devil's Lies

The devil's lies affect you much more than you realize. One of the devil's main jobs is to keep you in the dark concerning his operations – to keep you from being able to connect the dots so to speak. God wants you to be able to discern spirits, to be able to see into the spirit world, not with your physical eyes, but with the eyes of your spirit.

Your spirit is the very substance of who you really are. You are a spirit, you have a soul, which is your mind and emotions, and you live in your earth suit, your body. There is only one way that anyone can get here on earth; they must be born into it in an earth suit. When our earth suit wears out or gets fatally hurt, our spirit and soul have to return to the Father. The reason devils want to inhabit and or control us is because they don't have an earth suit and the only way they can have any control here is to have one, so they want yours.

The devil was firmly entrenched in my family which is why I was so open to the evil supernatural. He is firmly entrenched in many families bringing curses from one generation to the next. We can either choose to enter into these curses or choose to be obedient and enter into God's blessings.

"Behold, I set before you this day a blessing and a curse: A blessing, if ye obey the commandments of the Lord your God, which I command you this day: and a curse, if ye will not obey the commandments of the Lord your God, but turn aside out of the way which I command you this day, to go after other gods, which ye have not known" (Deuteronomy 11:26-28).

If you have involved yourself in any sin or opened any doors in your life then it is important that you clear up any legal grounds (or strongholds) that you gave the enemy relating to a curse or bondage before casting spirits out. I believe unforgiveness is a great way to open the doors to generational spirits and spirits of sin to come in. Do not allow bitterness or unforgiveness in your heart. Unforgiveness is a serious sin that blocks the forgiveness of your own sins and gives legal grounds for the enemy to operate in your life. Remember, forgiveness is a decision, not a feeling.

"But if ye forgive not men their trespasses, neither will your Father forgive your trespasses" (Matthew 6:15.

The Road to Deliverance

Start to confess what is rightfully yours. You have been redeemed from the law of sin and death. There is power in our confessions. Get out your list and go down that list one by one and confess every generational curse and every sin of disobedience to God. There is a legal process whereby you can be delivered and redeemed from the curse of the law and any demonic bondage in your life. This is the road to deliverance: It consists of five very important steps. 1) Recognize, 2) renounce, 3) confess, 4) bless, and 5) cast out.

Recognize: If the problem is demonic and recognize how ground was given and doors opened. Ask the Holy Spirit, He will help in this process.

Renounce: The problems as lies of the devil. Renounce the lies and the situations that gave ground and opened doors. Renounce them one by one.

"Neither give place to the devil.
Let him that stole steal no more: but rather let him labour, working with his hands the thing which is good that he may have to give to him that needeth.

Let no corrupt communication proceed out of your mouth, but that which is good to the use of edifying, (building up) that it may minister grace unto the hearers" (Ephesians 4:27-29).

"Therefore seeing we have this ministry, as we have received mercy, we faint not (do not become discouraged);

But have renounced the hidden things of dishonesty" (2 Corinthians 4:1,2a).

Confess: Confess the promise in God's Word that states your situation, as it *should* be. Decree it and it shall be established.

"Thou shalt also decree a thing, and it shall be established unto thee: and the light shall shine upon thy ways" (Job 22:28).

Then, the next step is to replace the lie with the truth by finding Scriptures in the concordance in the back of your Bible that are opposite of the sin. For example, if you are renouncing the sin of lust, use the following Scripture against the devil:

"Flee also youthful lusts: but follow righteousness, faith, charity, (love) peace, with them that call on the Lord out of a pure heart" (2 Timothy 2:22).

Bless: Those who may have proclaimed curses on you. They must be blessed one by one by name. Then, it is important to forgive them.

"Bless them that curse you, and pray for them which despitefully use you" (Luke 6:28).

Forgive them with an act of your will, even if they are no longer living. The story in the book of Judges is a perfect example of why we are to bless those that curse us.

"And there was a man of mount Ephraim, whose name was Micah. And he said unto his mother, the eleven hundred shekels of silver that were taken from thee, about which thou cursedst, and spakest of also in mine ears, behold, the silver is with me; I took it. And his mother said, blessed be thou of the Lord, my son" (Judges 17:1, 2).

That man's mother knew how to break a curse. She knew that it would be broken by blessing her son whom she had previously unknowingly cursed.

Cast Out: After lying the foundation, cast out the spirits one by one. You can do this very quietly. It is not necessary to yell or scream. God is not deaf and neither is the devil!

There are Scriptural benefits from following this process. Satan's access to your life is removed. The deliverance is much more likely to be permanent, providing you will obey God and not re-open the door by re-committing sin. Remember that Jesus said,

"IF you continue in My Word, THEN you shall know the truth and the truth shall make you free" (John 8:31, 32).

Submit yourselves therefore to God. Resist the devil, and he will flee from you" (James 4:7).

The following is a prayer you can pray while going through this five step process:

Father, I ask you to forgive me for my sins and cleanse me from any area where I have allowed the devil to enter into my life. I renounce all involvement with the works of the devil and darkness. In the name of Jesus I now cancel and break every curse because I have been redeemed from the curse. I will to forgive the people who have spoken against me so that curses will no longer operate in my life. I ask you to cover me and my family with your protection.

Now, to stay free you can memorize and claim the following blood promises every day.

BLOOD PROMISES

My sins are forgiven by the Blood of Jesus.
I am redeemed by the Blood of Jesus,
out of the hand of Satan.
I am justified and made righteous
by the Blood of Jesus.
The Blood of Jesus protects me from all evil.
I belong to Jesus Christ, God's Son,
spirit, soul and body.
Because of the Blood of Jesus,
Satan has no more power over me
No more place in me.
Jesus said, "These signs shall follow
them that believe,
In My Name they shall cast out devils."
I am a believer,
And in the Name of Jesus,
devil, I cast you out!

CHAPTER **22**

Is Jesus the Only Way?

How Can Christians Be So Sure?

YOU HAVE PROBABLY heard Christians say that Jesus is the only way to God and the only way to heaven. There just isn't any other way. But how can Christians be so sure? It may seem unfair, unjust, or even prideful for Christians to say that Jesus is the only way that a person can have a relationship with God but when you come to a true understanding of who God really is, you won't have to figure it out in your intellect, you will know in your spirit that Jesus definitely is the only way. Christians say that Jesus is the only way to God because that is what He said. It is Jesus' claim, not something we just came up with. It is what the Bible says.

Is The Bible Really the Word of God?

Christians know that Jesus is the only way because the Bible says so. But, you say, the Bible is just a book. No, the Bible is not just an ordinary book. It is the inspired Word of God. In fact, it is a collection of 66 inspired books. These books contain history, poetry, prophecy, wisdom literature, and so much more. They were written by 40 different authors who came from all kinds of backgrounds. They were shepherds, fishermen, doctors, kings, prophets, and hardly any of them knew one another.

The reason these men did not know one another is because these 66 books were written over a period of 1500 years so there was no way they could have worked together. Yet amazingly, these men managed to come up with similar themes throughout the entire Bible.

These authors wrote their books in three different languages. The Old Testament was first written in the Hebrew language, and the New Testament was written in the Greek and Aramaic languages. Now to make matters even more interesting, let me tell you that these 66 books were written on three different continents: Africa, Asia, and Europe.

So, now we have 66 books, written by 40 different authors, over 1500 years, in three different languages, on 3 different continents. Yet they all have a common story to tell: the creation, the fall, and the redemption of mankind. The entire Bible is the story of how God loves us and wants to redeem us out of the hands of the devil. It is the story of how redemption (salvation) is available to whosoever will repent of their sins and follow the Lord Jesus Christ.

"For whosoever shall call upon the name of the Lord shall be saved" (Romans 10:13).

From Genesis to Revelation it is for people in every generation. It was relevant for those who lived in Jesus' day and it is as relevant for us today as it was to them back then.

PART 3: SPIRITUAL WARFARE

"Jesus Christ the same yesterday, and today, and forever" (Hebrews 13:8).

God's Love Letter

Before you cried out to God to save you the Bible might not have made much sense. It is like reading someone else's mail – their love letters - but when you invite Jesus into your heart and into your life asking Him to forgive your sins, you become the object of His affection. That is when your spiritual eyes are opened and you will believe that the Bible is the Word of God. You believe it because God Himself impresses it in your spirit. It begins to make perfect sense and speak directly to you. This is what it says about Jesus being the only way:

"Jesus saith unto him, I am the way, and the truth, and the life; no man cometh unto the Father, but by Me" (John 14:6).

"Neither is there salvation in any other; for there is none other name under heaven given among men, whereby we must be saved" (Acts 4:12).

"For there is one God, and one mediator between God and men, the man Christ Jesus" (1 Timothy 2:5).

But I am already religious, you might say. Being religious cannot save you. In the book of John we see Jesus speaking to the religious, but unbelieving, Pharisees and explaining:

"I said therefore unto you, that ye shall die in your sins: for if ye believe not that I am He, ye shall die in your sins.

Then said they unto Him, who art thou? And Jesus saith unto them, Even the same that I said unto you from the beginning.

I have many things to say and to judge of you; but He that sent Me is true: and I speak to the world those things which I have heard of Him.

They understood not that he spake to them of the Father" (John 8:24-27).

Jesus Paid our Death Sentence

We were sentenced to death because of our sin. You see, everyone is separated from God by their sin and needs to be forgiven. The penalty for sin is death but Jesus paid the penalty for our sin when He died on the cross. Only death can pay the death penalty for sin.

"As it is written, there is none righteous, no, not one" (Romans 3:10).

"For all have sinned and come short of the glory of God" (Romans 3:23).

"For the wages of sin is death; but the gift of God is eternal life through Jesus Christ our Lord" (Romans 6:23).

"For whosoever shall call upon the name of the Lord shall be saved" (Romans 10:13).

"But as many as received Him, to them gave He power to become the sons of God, even to them that believe on His name;

Which were born, not of blood, nor of the will of the flesh, nor of the will of man, but of God" (John 1:12, 13).

Salvation is available but it is not automatic. Each one of us must ask for God's forgiveness, will to forgive others, and invite Jesus to come in. Each one of us must believe and receive Him and what He accomplished for us at His crucifixion. Jesus was the only One who was able to do this because He was fully God and He was fully man, a sinless man. On the cross, God judged Jesus for our sin so that we would not be judged and not be declared to be guilty. That is why He is the only way to God. Only Jesus was willing and able to die for us to pay our death penalty, and provide forgiveness for your sins. No other religious leader has done this and no other could have done this.

So, now the choice is ours. We either choose to pay the penalty for sin, eternal life without God – eternity in hell, or we can choose to allow Jesus to pay the price for us by accepting Him. When we consider the sacrifice He made for us, it is easy to see that there is only one way. We need to be thankful to God that He has so graciously providing any way at all.

When I was delivered out of the darkness of witchcraft into God's marvelous light, I was so grateful that the God of the universe is a GOOD God! I had a taste of what hell must be like with all the demonic harassment and torment I suffered. What if the god of the universe really was Satan I thought? What a horrible state of affairs that would be.

You've Come a Long Way Baby!

"But ye are a chosen generation, a royal priesthood, a

holy nation, a peculiar people; that ye should show forth the praises of Him who hath called you out of darkness into His marvelous light" (2 Peter 2:9).

Pretty awesome isn't it? You are now part of a royal priesthood! You sure have changed!

Some people might say that Christianity is too narrow and only narrow minded people believe in it. Just because something is narrow does not mean that it is wrong. An airport runway is pretty narrow and it is narrow to think that the plane you are traveling in should land right side up and on the narrow runway, but it is right. Math is pretty narrow too. 6 plus 6 is always going to be 12, narrow as that may be, it is still right.

There are other religions that claim to be the only way, but all religions cannot be the only way because they are in disagreement with one another. Christianity says that the way to salvation is Jesus and that it is a free gift that you cannot work for. Every other religion says that salvation is not a gift and that it has got to be earned by doing good works and deeds. Only one of those claims can be true, salvation is either a free gift from God or you have to be a good person to earn it. How good must you be? When would you know when you have been good enough? No, Jesus gives us His goodness and His righteousness.

Jesus IS God

Jesus not only said He was the only way to God when He was here on earth, but He even claimed to BE God! Then He rose from the dead. There is more evidence for His resurrection than any event in ancient history. When you realize that Buddha Confucius, Mohammed, and all the other religious leaders of the past are still in their tombs, it becomes clear that, indeed, Jesus is the only one who is still alive. Yes, He is alive!

Then there are those who will say, "As long as you are sincere, what you believe doesn't matter." Now you know that can't be true. Believing sincerely that something is true does not make it true. I can sincerely believe that I can flip a switch and the lights will go on when I haven't paid the bill in months. I can sincerely believe that when I turn the ignition in my car that it will go even if I haven't put gas in the gas tank since the gas gauge said empty. I can sincerely believe that this new diet where I eat 6000 calories a day will cause me to lose weight – but guess what – none of those things are true no matter how sincere I was in believing them.

So, what is really true? Does it really matter what you believe? Is the way to heaven paved with sincerity, goodness, and belief in God? Or is Jesus really the only way, the truth and the life? Maybe I just need to keep the Ten Commandments – oh really? How many of them do you have to keep? Did you ever steal anything? Did you ever break a Sabbath, used God's name in cursing someone or something? Have you ever dishonored your parents? Looked longingly at someone with lust in mind? Then you have broken all of them.

The Ten Commandments cannot possibly be kept by us humans. Actually, what they do is show us how hopeless it is to even try. Without Jesus having died for all the times we didn't keep the Commandments, past, present, and future, we would spend eternity in hell.

The bottom line is that the choice is ours. No one else can make our choice for us. We either choose to accept Him or reject Him. Remember that not making a choice is really making the choice to reject Him. We alone will stand before

◄ REDEEMING HARD TIME AND HARD TIMES

Almighty God someday and answer the question He will ask, "Why should I let you spend eternity with Me in my heaven?" What will your answer be? I pray that you will say something like, "Sir, because I am Your child. I have accepted that You, the Father, have judged the Son for my sin and I have been set free and now I belong to You!

CHAPTER **23**

Know So Hope

NOW, IF YOU have begun to read your Bible you have also come to realize that it is authentic, real, true, and relevant for all Christians in every age, and that means for us living today as well. In reading the Bible you will see that there is no need of depression and hopelessness because Jesus has your back. You are not left hopeless, no matter what your circumstances may be, you can hope in the plan that He has for your life.

Behind Bars or Behind the Eight Ball

Perhaps you are thinking; how can I walk in God's plan if I am behind bars for the rest of my life? How can I live out God's plan if I am confined to a wheel chair for the rest of my life? What does life hold for me if I have messed it up so bad that there is no hope for my future? That is what is sometimes referred to as being behind the eight ball. Being behind the eight ball is a weak, losing position in the game of pool or in life. It is a difficult, disadvantageous and very un-comfortable position to be in. You don't want to be in this situation, because it makes it seem as though it is impossible to win. If you have ever played the game of pool, you will know that being behind the eight ball means the game is over! But now that you belong to Jesus your impossible situation has changed. Your future has just begun! This is what Jesus says about a being in an impossible situation:

"But Jesus beheld them, and said unto them, with men this is impossible; but with God all things are possible" (Matthew 19:26).

"For with God nothing shall be impossible" (Luke 1:37).

"And being fully persuaded that what He had promised, He was able also to perform" (Romans 4:21).

You see, life is more than just a game of pool; it is the beginning to your eternity. There is hope for your future whether that future is spent in a seemingly impossible situation or spent living a good life. Even a good life will get better with Jesus and then you will spend eternity in heaven with Him. What a deal!

"There is hope in thine end (your future) saith the Lord, that thy children shall come again to their own border" (Jeremiah 31:17).

You might be thinking that the search for hope is too difficult, and you have given up trying to find it. Make no mistake about it, there is a hope for your future, and not only yours, but your children's' future as well. You see, when you get right with God good things will happen for your kids too. Now you must admit, that is good news!

God is Love

Why would God love such sinners as we? Because He IS love.

"He that loveth not knoweth not God; for God is love:" (1 John 4:8).

You know how it feels to be in love. It is a fabulous "high" better than any drug you have ever taken, especially when you know that the object of your love loves you back. But think about it, God loves us no matter what - even when we didn't love Him. His love for us will never change. God will never "fall out of love" with you. Now that should give you hope!

"Behold, what manner of love the Father hath bestowed upon us that we should be called the sons of God; therefore the world knoweth us not, because it knew Him not.
Beloved, now we are the sons of God, and it doth not yet appear what we shall be: but we know that, when He shall appear, we shall be like Him for we shall see Him as He is.
And every man that hath this hope in Him purifieth himself, even as He is pure" (1 John 3:1-3).

Our Blessed Hope

So, now you know there is hope for your present and hope for your immediate future, but just exactly what is this hope for the future that we have in Him? The Apostle Paul calls it our "blessed hope" – the glorious appearing of our God and Savior, the Lord Jesus Christ.

What is meant by "His appearing," does it mean He is coming back? That is exactly what it means. Jesus is coming back to gather up His people. Christians have this hope inside of them. It is a heart expectation and longing for His glorious appearing that you will learn about in the next chapter.

Christian hope is not just an illusion or some false hope, rather, it is a precious inheritance that is yet to be revealed. The Bible tells us how we, as Christians, have a living hope, not an "I hope so" but a hope that we can count on. A hope that will not disappoint us, a hope that is so certain and real that the Apostle Paul tells us that we can rejoice when we are in tribulations and troubles because it is only for a little while and can't even be compared with the glorious future that awaits us.

"Blessed be the God and Father of our Lord Jesus Christ, which according to His abundant mercy hath begotten us again unto a lively hope by the resurrection of Jesus Christ from the dead.

To an inheritance incorruptible, and undefiled, and that fadeth not away, reserved in heaven for you,

Who are kept by the power of God through faith unto salvation ready to be revealed in the last time" (1 Peter 1:3-5).

Present Trials

"Wherein ye greatly rejoice, though now for a season, if need be ye are in heaviness through manifold temptations;

That the trial of your faith, being much more precious than of gold that perisheth, though it be tried with fire, might be found unto praise and honor and glory at the appearing of Jesus Christ:

PART 3: SPIRITUAL WARFARE

Whom having not seen, ye love; in whom, though now ye see Him not, ye believing, ye rejoice with joy unspeakable and full of glory;
Receiving the end of your faith, even the salvation of your souls" (1 Peter 1:4-9).

"For I reckon that the sufferings of this present time are not worthy to be compared with the glory which shall be revealed in us" (Romans 8:18).

So, you see, there is something much greater involved here than just becoming a Christian and there is also something much greater involved in suffering. We have something the world without Christ does not have…our suffering is temporary, but our eternity with Jesus is forever.

Hope in the life of anyone is very powerful. Without it you will be depressed, emotionally exhausted, disoriented, and incapacitated. Hope energizes you and helps you cope with everyday life. It helps you cope with everyday life without drugs, alcohol, gambling, sexual pleasures outside of marriage, crime, just to name of few of the things that hold individuals in bondage without Christ. Hope has the power to completely change the entire direction of a Christian's life. The kind of hope we have is not the I hope so kind but the I know so kind.

"For we are saved by hope; but hope that is seen is not hope; for what a man seeth, why doth he yet hope for:
But if we hope for that we see not, then do we with patience wait for it" (Romans 8:24, 25).

We were given this hope when we were saved. If we

already have something we don't need to hope for it do we? But if we look forward to something we don't yet have, we must wait patiently for it and really believe it will come to pass. How wonderful to be able to have faith, patience and hope for the Kingdom of God that we know is soon to be revealed.

CHAPTER **24**

The Rapture of the Church

Is Jesus Really Coming Back?

ALL YOU HAVE to do is read the newspapers or watch the news programs on television to see Bible prophecy being fulfilled before your very eyes. There have been more prophecies fulfilled in the twentieth century than in any other time in history. It shows us that the time is rapidly approaching for the Lord Jesus Christ to return to this earth and take the kingdoms of this world for Himself.

Before this event occurs, the Second Coming of Christ, the Bible speaks of another event, a literal sudden return of the Lord Jesus Christ in the clouds to catch away the living saints (Christians are referred to as saints in the New Testament). Yes, imagine that, if you have received Christ, you are a saint! At a split second before the living Christians are caught up, He will also resurrect the Christians who have already died.

"For the Lord Himself shall descend from heaven with a shout, with the voice of the archangel, and with the trump of God; and the dead in Christ shall rise first;

Then we which are alive and remain shall be caught up together with them in the clouds, to meet the Lord in the air; and so shall we ever be with the Lord.
Wherefore comfort one another with these words" (1 Thessalonians 4:16-18).

The event described here by the Apostle Paul in these verses is often referred to as the Rapture of the Church. The term "rapture" comes from the Latin work *raptus*, which means caught away.

But when will this event take place? Jesus, when He was on earth, gave several warning signs, things that would happen previous to the Rapture. He did not give an exact date, in fact He said that no man knows the day or the hour. The Bible does say one thing that will happen is that evil men and imposters will grow worse and worse.

"But evil men and seducers shall wax worse and worse, deceiving and being deceived" (1 Timothy 3:13).

As society becomes more and more wicked, it becomes more and more clear that God will reach a point where He decides to punish the evil in the earth. Jesus said some things when He was here on earth that we need to be aware of concerning the last days before the Rapture.

"And as He sat upon the Mount of Olives, the disciples came unto Him privately, saying; tell us, when shall these things be? And what shall be the sign of Thy coming, and of the end of the world?
And Jesus answered and said unto them, Take heed that no man deceive you.

For many shall come in My name, saying, I am Christ, and shall deceive many.

And ye shall hear of wars and rumors of wars: see that ye be not troubled; for all these things must come to pass, but the end is not yet.

For nation shall rise against nation, and kingdom against kingdom; and there shall be famines, and pestilences, and earthquakes, in divers places.

All of these are the beginning of sorrows" (Matthew 24:4-8).

What You Have Learned So Far

Let's back track here a little and take a look at what we have covered so far. You learned what Christianity is and why you need to make the choice to follow the Lord Jesus Christ. You have learned what it means to be born again and how to be delivered from evil spirits. You also learned that you are a new creature now that you are in Christ. You have learned what forgiveness is and what it is not and why it is necessary to forgive others, and more importantly, how to forgive yourself. We talked about stinkin' thinkin and most important of all, you learned that there is a war going on in the heavenlies and that you are prime target number one now that you are saved. Gee thanks, you might say.

Well, actually, you were prime target number one before you were a born again Christian in the Kingdom of God. But, the difference was that you didn't have a lot of Scripture in you and as a result your worldview was not changed for the better and you didn't even realize that there was a war going on. You were playing right into the devil's hand. In part 3 of this book you not only learned you were in a war, you learned how to effectively use the weapons of that warfare to kick the devil out of your life.

You learned that you have been redeemed out of the hands of the devil and you are now in the hands of Almighty God. If it was power you were looking for, you now have the greatest power in the universe at your disposal. So, you might be thinking, now what, where do I go from here?

The Icing on the Cake

No cake is complete unless it has icing on it and please forgive me if I equate Christianity with a cake, but there is no sweeter experience than being a Christian. I call the Rapture of the Church, the icing. We get born again, live a great life for the Lord, and then we get to go with Him when He comes to gather up all His kids!

When you consider the times in which we live there can be no question that something strange is going on all around us. You see, the Bible foretells this event that will absolutely stun the world. It is an event that will happen suddenly and without warning. Actually, it can happen at any moment now. The word "Rapture" isn't in the Bible but the concept is certainly there. The prophets, apostles, and Jesus Himself have listed several signs that will happen just before this strange event takes place.

When Jesus was on earth around two thousand years ago He warned of signs that would come upon mankind just before the Rapture. He said that no one knows exactly when this will take place, but that it most certainly will.

"But of that day and hour knoweth no man, no not the angels of heaven, but My Father only.

But as the days of Noah were, so shall also the coming of the Son of man be.

For as in the days that were before the flood they were eating and drinking, marrying and giving in marriage, until the day that Noah entered into the ark,

And knew not until the flood came, and took them all away; so shall also the coming of the Son of man be.

Then shall two be in the field; the one shall be taken, and the other left.

Two women shall be grinding at the mill; the one shall be taken, and the other left.

Watch therefore: for ye know not what hour your Lord doth come.

But know this, that if the goodman of the house (the head of the household) had known in what watch the thief would come, he would have watched, and would not have suffered (allowed) his house to be broken up.

Therefore be ye also ready: for in such an hour as ye think not the Son of man cometh" (Matthew 24:36-44).

Signs of the Times

The Apostle Paul gives us more insight into how the world will be when Jesus returns.

"This know also, that in the last days perilous times shall come.

For men shall be lovers of their own selves, covetous, boasters, proud, blasphemers, disobedient to parents, unthankful, unholy.

Without natural affection, trucebreakers, false accusers, incontinent (unable to control themselves), fierce, despisers of those that are good,

REDEEMING HARD TIME AND HARD TIMES

Traitors, heady, highminded, lovers of pleasures more than lovers of God:

Having a form of godliness, but denying the power thereof: from such turn away" (2 Timothy 3:1-5).

These verses give us a very graphic view of the evil that will be prevalent in the world when it is near the time of Jesus' return. We all have been victims, to some extent, to this ungodliness that is going on all around us these days. You can see by some of these descriptions that most of them relate to and focus directly on self. No doubt this is the "me generation" where everything seems to revolve around the self. It is easy to see that self-satisfaction and instant gratification are driving forces in the world today.

Sex is an area where this driving force of self-gratification is extremely obvious. Sex is an area that has been created by God for reproduction and bonding in the marriage relationship. Fornication is sex outside of marriage and is forbidden by God, yet more and more promiscuity and perverted sexual behavior has become the norm in our society. We have adopted the ungodly attitude of "if it feels good to me, it's okay" no matter what God says. The wedding vows are no long taken seriously and marriages are destroyed because of selfishness.

As you can see Jesus laid out several things that would be signals that the end times were upon us. He talked about there being wars and rumors of wars, false prophets and false teachers. He spoke of ethnic hatred, starvation, disease and earthquakes in many places. He also foretold that the tiny country of Israel would be at the center of the world's attention which it is today.

You might say there have always been wars, and false prophets. There has always been ethnic hatred, starvation, disease, and there have always been earthquakes. But what Jesus was prophesying, however, was that all these things, and more, would increase in frequency and intensity as the time of His coming was drawing near.

The Tribulation

But why does there need to be a Rapture of the Church you might be asking? The reason there needs to be a gathering together and a removal from the earth of God's people is because there is also going to be a Tribulation. It will be a seven year period of time that will bring horrible judgment on the people who have refused to accept the free gift of salvation. They have refused to receive the gift of the death of Jesus on the cross, His burial and His resurrection as payment for their sin. You see, sin cannot enter heaven. It is what separates us from God and it is why we need to be born again, born the second time spiritually, so that we can be cleansed from sin and so we will be ready for this gathering that will take us to be with Jesus in heaven.

People who live for Jesus Christ have eternal life and are not going to be judged for sin. God sees those who are born again as perfect and sinless, just the way Adam and Eve were before they sinned in the Garden of Eden. Make no mistake about it; we are all going to life forever somewhere, either in heaven or hell. God has given that choice to us. He doesn't send anyone to hell, but He loves mankind enough to allow him to make his own choices about where he wants to spend eternity. He also doesn't force heaven on anyone. Eternity in heaven is also our choice. People who have not accepted Jesus Christ as their Lord and Savior will be left behind to face God's judgment on earth during the Tribulation.

The only thing that is holding back the evil to come is the Holy Spirit in us, the saints of God. It is His restraint upon the evil in the world that is holding back wickedness. When we are taken out of the way the Antichrist can be revealed. Once the Rapture takes place demonic activity will exceed our wildest imaginations.

The Second Coming

This is an event that will take place at the end of the seven year Tribulation. Jesus Christ will return with the Church (that's us) to defeat the antichrist who will be the devil in the flesh. He will overthrow evil and then establish His thousand year reign which is referred to as the Millennium.

Jesus, who is God, came first to the earth as a humble baby boy, born to a poor family in a stable. But the next time He comes it will be as the King of all kings. Revelation is the very last book in the Bible and is the book that most specifically prophesies what the end time is going to look like. It speaks of an apocalyptic period of time with widespread destruction and devastation, the likes of which have never been known before. It also speaks of the one thousand years that will follow when we will be reigning with Jesus in the New Jerusalem. I challenge you to read the book of Revelation along with the rest of the Bible so you can see for yourself that you entered into a new dimension when you received Jesus Christ as your Lord and Savior.

The Resurrection of Life and the Resurrection of Damnation

"Blessed and holy is he that hath part in the first resurrection: on such the second death hath no power, but they shall

be priests of God and of Christ, (that's us) and shall reign with him a thousand years" (Revelation 20:6).

This is the good, or *"first resurrection,"* at the start of the 1000 years. Those in it need not fear the second death. But there will also be a bad or second resurrection, at the conclusion of the 1000 years. Jesus Christ called it *"the resurrection of damnation."*

"And shall come forth; they that have done good, unto the resurrection of life; and they that have done evil, unto the resurrection of damnation" (John 5:29).

So as you can see Jesus is not the only one who will be resurrected. You will be also. These Scriptures make it plain that people will be involved in two resurrections - one at the beginning of the Millennium, in which true believers in Christ are raised to eternal life; and one at the opposite end of the Millennium, in which the *"unjust"* awake to something else entirely. Surely you don't want to be in that second resurrection of damnation for all eternity. Those who are not caught up when Jesus comes will be destroyed.

Your Mansion Awaits

What about God's people? What about those who participated in the first resurrection of life and who were caught up with Jesus as opposed to being left behind? What happens to them during the Millennium? Near the end of His earthly ministry, Jesus told His followers that He was going to heaven, where He would be preparing mansions for His children.

"Let not your heart be troubled: ye believe in God, believe also in me.

In my Father's house are many mansions: if it were not so I would have told you. I go to prepare a place for you.

And if I go and prepare a place for you, I will come again, and receive you unto myself; that where I am there ye may be also" (John 14:1-3).

And what will we be doing there in heaven with God? We will be reigning with Him forever and ever.

"And there shall be no night there; and they need no candle, neither light of the sun; for the Lord God giveth them light; and they shall reign forever and ever" (Revelation 20:23).

We will be in some position of authority, just as Adam originally reigned over the earth and had dominion.

New Heaven and New Earth

The 20th chapter of the book of Revelation ends with these solemn words:

"Whosoever was not found written in the book of life was cast into the lake of fire" (Revelation 20:15).

"And I, (John) saw a new heaven and a new earth: for the first heaven and the first earth were passed away; and there was no more sea" (Revelation 21:1).

New heaven and new earth! What happened to the old

ones? They were destroyed. The Apostle Peter explains that it will all be destroyed by fire.

"Looking for and hasting unto the coming of the day of God, wherein the heavens being on fire shall be dissolved, and the elements shall melt with fervent heat?
Nevertheless we, according to His promise. Look for new heavens and a new earth, wherein dwelleth righteousness" (2 Peter 3:12:13).

God completely purifies this planet and its atmosphere. He will recreate the earth and the sky and cleanse them from the contamination of sin.

"And God will wipe away all tears from their eyes; and there shall be no more death, neither sorrow nor crying, neither shall there be any more pain; for the former things are passed away.
And He that sat upon the throne said, behold, I make all things new and He said unto me, write; for these words are true and faithful" (Revelation 21:4, 5).

God told John to write, because these words are true. When these things finally happen, death, hell, sin, sorrow, crying and pain will have also passed away because they are the former things that John was referring to. There will be no more fear of terrorists, no more natural disasters, sickness, disease, divorce, or abuse.
When the destruction was over Noah and his family walked out of the ark onto dry land and into a cleansed, purified world. Just as Noah did, so shall we, God's faithful ones, finally step out of the New Jerusalem into a newly recreated world.

God is Pleading with You

You will be on one side or the other. You will either be deceived by the devil or you will accept the truth of the Gospel of Jesus Christ. You will either be caught up to be with the Lord and spend eternity with Him or you will be part of the destruction that is to come and spend eternity in hell with the devil and his hordes. There is no middle ground. Don't put off making your decision because Jesus could come at any moment.

Jesus died for you! He died so that you could have a place with Him in that New Jerusalem and in the new heavens and new earth that are coming. Your final destiny, inside or outside, eternal life or eternal destruction, depends upon YOUR choice. Will you give yourself to the One who gave Himself for you, and have eternity with Him, or will you continue resisting Him?

It is all going to happen. We can't change what has been prophesied and by the condition the world is in it looks as though the time is very short indeed. But you have the power to make the decision to choose Jesus Christ right now, before it's too late.

Examine Your Heart

I challenge you to examine your heart. What is your relationship with the Lord Jesus Christ? Is He your Savior? That's great, but He needs to be the Lord of your life as well. Don't be compromising, worldly, backslidden, and or lukewarm when it comes to your eternity. Make sure you are ready for the Rapture, ready for the day that Jesus comes in the clouds to gather those who belong to Him. Make the choice today that you will be counted in that number and pray this prayer.

PART 3: SPIRITUAL WARFARE

Dear Lord,

All the signs are pointing to your soon return. The evidence is that it could be any day now. I ask you to examine my heart, my life, my thoughts, my words, my actions, and even my motives. I desire to be ready for that day when You come for your own.

Even though I know that my sin has already been forgiven, I want to please you so I ask that you shine the light of your Holy Spirit on any area in my life that needs to change, any area in my life where I am in sin, be it in my flesh, in my thoughts, or even in my unconscious and or subconscious mind. In Jesus name I pray. Amen.

For those of you who still have not become a born-again Christian and would like to receive the free gift of salvation and escape from all the coming destruction, pray this prayer as well.

Lord Jesus,

I am a sinner and I acknowledge and confess my sins before You. I desire to turn away from my sin and turn to you to surrender. I believe you died to save me and you are coming soon. I turn my live over to you completely and ask you to come into my heart and into my life. I want to change, I want to turn away from the lies of the devil and become your child. I ask you to prepare my heart for your soon return. Thank you Lord. I pray this in Jesus name. Amen.

Welcome my friend into the most wonderful family in the universe. You are loved.

Citations & Resources

Caring People Recovery Center
5207 Mason Dixon Avenue
Bowling Green, FL 33834
863-375-3377

Charles & Frances Hunter
Hunter Ministries Kingswood, TX

History Channel – Armageddon Week
History Channel – Countdown to Armagedden
History Channel – Doomsday 2012. The End of Days

Holy Bible - King James Version

Mark Driscoll: Pastor of Mars Hill Church Seattle, WA

Skillings Mining Review, Duluth, MN

Teen Challenge International

Tyler Perry Play: Madea's Class Reunion

Webster's Dictionary

CPSIA information can be obtained at www.ICGtesting.com
Printed in the USA
LVOW120329030212
266805LV00001B/39/P